THE AMERICAN LANDSCAPE

BAAS Paperbacks

General Editor: Philip John Davies, Reader in American Studies at De Montfort University

Associate Editor: George McKay, Senior Lecturer in Cultural Studies at the University of Central Lancashire

Published in association with the British Association for American Studies, this exciting series is destined to become an indispensable collection in American Studies. Each volume tackles an important area and is written by an accepted academic expert within the discipline. Books selected for the series are clearly written introductions designed to offer students definitive short surveys of key topics in the field.

Forthcoming titles in the series include:

The United States and European Reconstruction, 1945–1960
John Killick

Political Scandals in the USA
Robert Williams

Gender and Sexuality in Contemporary American Film
Jude Davies and Carol Smith

The American Landscape

STEPHEN F. MILLS

KEELEUNIVERSITY**PRESS**

© Stephen F. Mills, 1997

Keele University Press
22 George Square, Edinburgh

Typeset in Monotype Fournier by
Carnegie Publishing, Preston and
printed and bound in Great Britain

A CIP record for this book is available
from the British Library

ISBN 1 85331 179 0

The right of Stephen F. Mills to be identified
as the author of this work has been asserted
in accordance with the
Copyright, Designs and Patents Act (1988)

Contents

Introduction: America the Place   1

1. The Physical Environment   13

2. Cultural Landscapes: The Imperial Legacy   25

3. Cultural Landscapes of the West   45

4. Landscape Painting   56

5. Interpreting Landscape Images   71

6. Studying the Urban Landscape   94

7. Theme Parks and Heritage Landscapes   101

Conclusion: American Studies and the American Landscape   117

Suggestions for Further Reading   122

Index   143

Introduction:
America the Place

The United States of America is a major national security state, an economic giant and, with the demise of the Soviet Union, the sole surviving world power. For many people across the world, the USA is primarily that mix of hard work and quick money, the 'American Dream', so exalted on movie screens and television. As such, the USA has long been a major destination for both the upwardly mobile and the dispossessed of many nations. For those interested in studying the USA, initial focus usually plays upon the political system, that mix of the Old and New World precedents, within which society orders and manipulates its tensions. Given its economic wealth, however, it is hardly surprising that, for many, the distinguishing feature of the USA is not so much its political system, however fascinating are its election campaigns and its Watergate to Whitewater exposés, but its prodigious economic wealth and, hence, its impact upon world trade. A vast continental economy has emerged from a series of small British trading colonies to become an essential pivot within the modern world order. And it has been this growing reputation for economic wealth, once based in agriculture, then in industry, now in information, that has continued to induce so many people to make new lives here. America is its people, a vast human kaleidoscope where once there were only indigenous peoples. But America is more than a melting-pot: bundle all its various dimensions together and what emerges is America the place, a particular mixture of past and present, of peoples and their activities, that distinguishes the USA from all other countries.

A sense of place is, perhaps, the ultimate synthesis, the bringing together of all dimensions of environment, perception and experience into a vast whole. But to treat a sense of place as some ultimate interweaving of everything of significance within a particular country or region is to invite an unrealistic expectation. More realistically, notions of place can be used to focus upon specific aspects of the US experience.

A concern for place recognises that many of the great processes of political, social and economic life have left their mark upon the face of America – its landscape. One of America's distinguishing characteristics, therefore, is that it actually looks different from other countries. The peculiar mix of peoples that is America, that pragmatic mix of free enterprise and regulation that is the US economy, along with the organisation of the tensions between these various elements that is the American political system, all leave their mark upon America as a place. As places emerge, change, and sometimes even die, the landscape is often the only record of what has happened. Traces of past lives can be found embedded in the landscape long after even folk memories have faded away: learn to read the landscape and you too may see traces of people and events for which no other trace may exist. The landscape is a public record of all those forces that helped to fashion it, mould it, and even destroy it. The landscape is a memorial to America, but often an unintended one. Some areas have been deliberately sculpted to commemorate specific people or events, such as the Mall in Washington DC, with its array of presidential and military memorials, or the re-created Jamestown Settlement, to honour and explain the first English settlers of Virginia. Most of America, though, is an unwitting memorial to people and activities otherwise long since forgotten, ordinary life built into everyday surroundings.

This study of the American landscape has been written at a time of growing interest in the environment across a wide range of interests, whether amongst the general public or within academic circles. It seems appropriate, then, to mention one aspect that is crucial to the growing environmental debate: what is landscape? Such a question may initially appear trivial, pedantic, even 'academic', but far from being a self-evident term, 'landscape' is amazingly problematic. And as Americans come increasingly to debate what should happen to their landscapes, famous and mundane ideas as to what landscape is (and is not) are a crucial influence on public discussion. So this study will raise some general questions about landscape – an essential task, given that there are often quite rival notions as to what should be studied. The substantive focus explores the creation, interpretation and representation of US landscapes, looking in particular at the way in which landscape changes illuminate otherwise occluded aspects of the American experience.

What is landscape? This important question has been answered in many radically different, and possibly mutually exclusive, ways. Is it what's out there, an empirical reality, or a representation, a framed image of some aspect of reality? No two textbooks will agree.[1] Many protagonists insist on one meaning or the other, but rarely both. The two divergent schools of thought generally reflect two rival academic traditions: that of the environmental sciences, particularly geography, and that of the humanities, particularly art history. Only recently have there been explicit attempts to integrate these once traditional approaches, partly influenced by the recognition that popular views about landscape need to be taken on board, not ignored.

The textbook approach to landscape has traditionally consisted of an examination of environmental changes effected by human activity, starting with those background features of general relief, climate, vegetation and soils that existed prior to any human impact upon plants and animals. Physical geography is followed by the impact made by agriculture, trade and, finally, industry over the ensuing years, leading inevitably to contemporary landscape changes, with their varying cultural, technological and even ideological aspects.[2] Such an approach can be exceedingly encyclopaedic and frequently dull, no more riveting than old-fashioned geography textbooks in their litany of geology, soil types, extractive industries and crops. Fortunately, the study of landscape has moved far beyond such pedagogical fossils and today embraces a broad spectrum of conceptual and methodological approaches, involving architects, social psychologists, ecologists, historians, archaeologists and literary critics as well as geographers. Even the meaning of the term 'landscape' is not generally agreed upon. For many, especially in the USA 'landscape' remains synonymous with the whole of the natural, unaltered physical environment. Given the comparatively recent extension of industrialised society over the US frontier, and the vastness of the (almost) primeval areas that still survive in the west (especially in Alaska), it is hardly surprising that this is so. An important confusion evoked by the casual use of the term 'landscape' is apparent in its relationship to the term 'wilderness'. While geographers and historians now see landscape as the product of human activity, a social product, part of the collective human transformation of the world, others continue to see landscape as synonymous with pre-human terrain, wilderness. Sometimes this confusion is the result of ahistorical ignorance – wild, desolate areas are deemed pristine, Eden-like, even where they are the product of human activity, such as overgrazing or too much logging. Appalachia, for instance, is as forested today as it ever was, but its forest communities and mix of species are the result of long-established clearing followed by regrowth which never quite reproduced what had been there earlier. Appalachia is both a human landscape and a wilderness, even where it seems hardly settled.[3]

Part of this confusion within landscape's pedigree emerged from the diffusion of Romantic – indeed, Transcendentalist – notions of communing with nature. In the face of relentless modernity, spiritual renewal was supposedly most likely where the human impress was least evident. In the last century, the power that the new sciences had over people's imagination encouraged a reaction that valued the wild for seeming so untamed. With the growth of scientific environmentalist perspectives, many came to see variety in the landscape as the product of purely natural forces, whether relict features from the geological past, the product of current climatic and weathering processes, or some combination of these. In a continent where people can seem so irrelevant beneath a prairie sky, puny within an Arctic storm, or helpless in a desert drought, it was hardly surprising that landscape variety was explained in primarily physical terms: geology plus climate equals vegetation within the constraints of altitude. With vegetation as a convenient surrogate for these complex interacting variables, the study of landscape variation became little more than an exercise in biogeography. Few residents of New York City realise how human activity has shaped the landscapes of the nearby Catskill Mountains. Where regrowth soon covered once barren mountains, there was a temptation to see all such desolate and wild areas as virgin lands, despite the role of hunting and logging prior to tourism, never mind the earlier impact of fire in the hands of the native peoples.

Where this study deals with the specifically physical environment, it focuses upon the changing interpretations of human interaction with the land rather than primeval patterns and their subsequent human modifications. US regional geography, the history of environmental awareness, even the emergence of US landscape painting and photography, are, along with certain US architectural trends, only brought in as evidence of how wide and varied are the interests and concerns of those who are as engaged with geomorphology as with landscape photography, the archaeological site as the skyscraper. Landscape studies are increasingly written by those concerned to explore this multidisciplinary field. There are, of course, disciplinary specialists involved with aspects of the landscape: architects, painters and photographers, literary scholars who tease out landscape imagery from the printed word, archaeologists who examine the legacy of past land use, those who study the impact of economic activity upon the environment, and geomorphologists who examine how physical processes mould the land. Each is usually only concerned with a narrowly defined field. The geomorphologist, for instance, imagines away all the human impact to focus upon the impact of varying climatic regimes. To interrogate the landscape as something more than the physical environment, however, we need to find a procedure for integrating these various concerns, editing back in and weaving together the very 'noise' that each field attempts so studiously to edit out. In doing so, the worth of each perspective may be undervalued – even if fully appreciated – and, at worst, a particular discipline's contribution may be misunderstood. The risk is worth taking, for the integration of ideas and approaches from a variety of fields may help to re-establish interest amongst those who have shied away from the well-worn tramlines of existing areas of study, such as architectural history or landscape aesthetics. And if our eventual goal is to understand American society through the landscape that it creates, maintains and reworks, then we do need to develop ways of integrating the insights and enthusiasms of discrete fields of study. Attempts to be holistic, to incorporate a range of disciplines that touch upon America the place, risk being so extravagant in their claims they must surely disappoint, though the potentials and opportunities involved in interdisciplinary work parallel long-standing debates in the UK over the nature of American Studies (is it an *ad hoc* collection of any US topic, an amalgam of US topics, or something that transcends contributing fields to provide unique insights into American culture?).[4]

Landscape studies, however integrationist, remain as partial as any other field. They may throw previously occluded aspects of American society into relief, but, in doing so, they will no doubt obscure other possible concerns for American life, overemphasising those aspects of human experience that involve material remains at the expense of those that do not. Nevertheless, a study of the landscape, from whatever perspective, continues to remind us that the USA is at least as much a place as an idea. Though landscape studies are now at the cutting edge of cultural geography, the study of the landscape has been notoriously unfashionable, even though landscape issues have long been one of geography's traditional interests. The focus has traditionally been the countryside, so the landscape has not seemed as immediately relevant to young scholars in an era of increasingly urban living. One obvious response to this growing urban focus for modern life was simply to study towns and suburbs – and not merely as latter-day destroyers of landscape, but as landscapes of people's most immediate experience. Whether urban or rural, certain questions remain. Who created these landscapes in the first instance? How did some landscapes survive intact, while others changed beyond recognition? What landscape elements survive even when their surroundings change? Studies increasingly focus upon how landscapes have been regarded, honoured, neglected, and even how they have been studied. With its focus upon the cultural landscape, this book explores the physical and cultural surroundings that people find bequeathed to them, that they live within, change and leave behind, with particular regard for the images of these landscapes that they carry around with them.

So, already we have two contrasting – indeed, rival – uses of the term 'landscape': that which is natural and that which is human. These are not the only uses of the term, however. Landscape as a term remains a word in everyday use. It is therefore available for all, from whatever walk of life. Even within academic circles it is used by many disciplines. As a word in common currency, landscape students have little or no control over its use – unlike the situation in the hard sciences, where terms such as 'velocity' can be defined unambiguously. 'Landscape', however, defies all attempts at definition. Rather, landscape must be approached through a recognition of its many, varied and not always compatible uses. It is more than what nature left us, more than just the impact of human activity. As an analytical term, landscape is more than what can be identified, classified and mapped. It is more than what can be sketched, painted or photographed. Like the associated term 'region', it carries multiple layers of meaning. It is not just the environment, natural or built.[5] Landscape implies an active, two-way engagement between people and their surroundings. Landscape is a composition, a selection of part of those surroundings – if only because surroundings are 360°, and yet, for the human visitor, landscape is at most 180°. Even attempts to present the whole 360° panorama involve a selection beyond normal human capabilities.[6] Landscape, then, is a way of seeing the world. Even the most die-hard proponents of 'seeing it as it is' still look out from their own perspective, both locationally and culturally.

Why is there so little agreement about what landscape is? This is partly due to the term's use by such a wide range of people – painters, photographers, planners, architects (never mind academics). Most, however, would probably agree that landscape is less simply what's out there, and more a way of *seeing* what's out there. Certainly, there's something essentially visual involved, an arrangement of phenomena, whether natural or human, which is quite different from what gets classified, counted or mapped. So, landscape is more than the earth's surface configuration. It is a way of selecting certain features on the earth's surface in line with certain visual concerns. Landscape is a construction – indeed, a composition, in that it selects and highlights certain visual aspects of the environment. And if landscape is less bricks and mortar or rivers and mountains, and more a way of seeing them as part of our world, then we are soon drawn to consider how we have learned, individually and collectively, to see certain images as landscape. Even as Americans were creating their world, they were also creating their notion of landscape. Students of landscape are drawn to those broader historical structures and processes within which such attitudes and responses to the world have emerged. Just as certain groups were critically engaged in creating the political systems, economic structures and physical surroundings of first the American colonies and then the newly independent republic, so certain groups have been critically involved in creating specific ways of addressing and responding to nature, particularly the way in which it should be portrayed and represented as well as the way in which it should be exploited or preserved. It is these very images that not only reflect contemporary attitudes, but help to influence further involvement with the physical world. The image 'in here' comes to leave its traces in our impact 'out there'. The initial dichotomy between landscape as physical place or as cultural image dissolves away.[7]

The ambiguity of the term 'landscape' continues to cause confusion, however; so much so that many in search of neat scientific clarity have given up on the term, though it remains impossible to ignore, given its wide currency. This ambiguity can nevertheless be used to advantage, for it continually reminds us that landscape is both the subject and the object of human activity, neither one nor the other, but essentially an interdisciplinary mix, one that should be meat and drink to any American Studies programme based firmly in the humanities' concerns for exploring meaning and interpretation.

It is useful initially to prise apart the two traditions: landscape as environment and landscape as image. Once it has been outlined how these two differ, but yet remain in contact, the analysis will concentrate upon the built, or human, landscape, how it came about in its regional and local complexities, and only then move on to deal with how the landscape has been represented, whether in the printed word, the celluloid image and beyond, before returning to the urban landscape, the modern cityscape. The physical processes that have created and continue to modify the physical environment will not be investigated here. Rather, physical change and variety will be taken as a given, suitably explored elsewhere by others.[8] Our concern will be with the way in which the physical environment has been appropriated and perceived, exploring some of the complex interactions between the landscape as given, as made and as perceived. Once particular approaches are used in the light of previously alien traditions, the hostility between very different approaches turns out to be redundant.

In the early part of this century, many American scholars become concerned to record fading elements of the built environment, attempting to create a rigorous scientific synthesis of those elements which, together, seemed to distinguish a particular area, at least in terms of its pre-industrial heritage.[9] Each element, whether fields, fences or barns, was initially subject to the kind of detailed morphological analysis normally associated with archaeological findings. Then came the significance of each artefact: where it had come from, how it had changed, and, finally, how did it fit into the mosaic that was the cultural landscape of a particular region?[10] Whether or not this concern for regional distinctiveness was merely a form of rescue archaeology before the forces of 'progress' rolled over once rural (and thus truly 'American') areas remains debatable. Suffice it to say that this type of analysis was promoted as being rigorously scientific, on a par with the biologist who dissects, labels and catalogues parts the better to understand the whole. But such analyses could equally be reductive. Even where the parts were then put back together, the end product had the perspective of a snapshot, aerial photograph or map, the all-seeing image (a precursor of later satellite imageries) deemed all-knowing. Scenery – that is, a view from the front porch, the car window or the overlook – was not initially of interest, nor was there a concern for the artist's framed representation of such artefacts. Yet the tradition of fieldwork became well established within the study of landscape, with its concerns for arrays of artefacts, buildings, and property lines, whether in the field or, later, within the image. Parallel and often oblivious to these trends was the use of landscape in common parlance, which tended to take its understanding from painters rather than from social scientists. Landscape *was* popularly seen as scenery, something interesting, magnificent or sublime enough to be worthy of attention, not for itself, but for the emotional response that it generated. Interestingly, landscape enthusiasts brought up in the morphological tradition have gradually become aware that empirically defined elements (however well integrated) only deal with what is out there at a superficial level. The fact that people continued to build, maintain and value covered bridges, for instance, in areas which never saw enough snow to make their construction worthwhile, suggests that there were deeper meanings involved, not all subject to immediate empirical verification. Morphological studies that identify, count, record and map may be necessary, but they are insufficient to account for landscape, as they ignore the meanings that people invest in these forms which remain to be teased out. Only then can we discover why some landscapes are created and preserved, while others are resisted or changed. New England spires and village greens,[11] the Amish farm-lands,[12] and the ante-bellum plantations[13] all have a symbolic importance that would never be appreciated by merely counting farm posts or mapping land holdings. Even landscapes that seem aesthetically unappealing, such as each town's commercial strip, may nevertheless have a strong symbolic meaning for many people. The commercial strip, for instance, is seen as something essentially American by both locals and by visitors, detractors and promoters. It has come to symbolise at least part, if not all, of America just as much as an older image of the main street at the heart of any small community.

Whereas landscape painting or photography have tended, at least until pop art's arrival, to be overly concerned with worthy subjects (wondrous waterfalls or sublime mountain ranges), modern landscape studies, perhaps because of their morphological inheritance of measuring the commonplace, are willing to look at anything and everything, however tacky (Disney World or used-car lots, Dollywood or diners), worthy (Washington DC's federal triangle), or even both (Gettysburg's battlefield site). This, paradoxically, accords with a post-modernist willingness to invest anything with significance, to treat everything as a potential clue to meaning. The landscape student is as interested in what has been built around such sublime sights as Niagara Falls, Yosemite National Park or Yellowstone's 'Old Faithful' as in these spectacular landscapes themselves. Where the landscape artist might well have

edited out the passing railroad, and the photographer might deliberately secure a pylon-free vista (or create one with the appropriate
computer software), the landscape analyst is likely to question the logic
behind such omissions, while asking why society would permit these
mundane landscape elements to be erected around supposedly revered
landscapes.

Modern analyses seek to replicate neither of the traditional approaches, the morphological or the aesthetic, at the expense of each other.
Certainly, it will be accepted that the US landscape, as any other, has
emerged as something that, once created, has been both appropriated
and worked over. How the physical geography (what people variously
call the 'topography' or 'land-forms', plus the native flora and fauna)
came into being, whether intact by a creator or in an evolutionary fashion
over time, need not be explored here. Rather, what is of interest is how
the land, once created, has been used to reflect cultural perceptions,
choices and decisions. In this light, Yi-Fu Tuan sees landscape as 'somewhat analogous to the interior of the house, in that its totality reveals
purposes and ends that have directed human energy'.[14]

People, however, live and work within specific places rather than
within a landscape. The visible aspects of their surroundings are only
one part of their relationship with the world around them, and may be
far from being the most important relationship. Aesthetic considerations,
however important, are rarely more vital than making a living and
raising a family. Surroundings are an integral part of ordinary life, not
a discrete part of 'over there'. The insider cannot walk away from the
surroundings of everyday life, as can a visitor. For the resident insider,
the world is not a picture on a wall from which he or she can divert her
gaze. But images are important: with the power to re-create surroundings
comes the opportunity to impose certain images upon the world to the
exclusion of others. If the new republic is 'an Empire for Freedom', as
Jefferson believed, then building administrative offices is an opportunity
to build imperial structures into the fabric of every town, to be the future
surroundings of everyday life. The plethora of imperial names (Rome,
New York; Athens, Georgia) is matched by the classical porticoes of
county court-houses and universities. A particular image of America's
future became built into the landscape, classical elements that were
designed to be seen and to encourage certain reactions. Landscape
became place made manifest, the outward and visible signs of the processes that created it.

Notes

1. Pick up any two books with 'landscape' in the title and you may find two radically different uses of the term. Two randomly chosen are D. K. Adams and I. F. A. Bell (eds), *Literary Landscapes* (Manchester UP: Manchester, 1988), and Peter Hall and Ann Markusen (eds), *Silicon Landscapes* (Allen and Unwin: London, 1985). Neither book studies the landscape *per se*; rather, each uses the term metaphorically to suggest a general, wide-ranging area of study – one literary, one economic. On the other hand, even texts overtly examining the landscape, such as W. G. Hoskins's classic, *The Making of the English Landscape* (Hodder and Stoughton: London, 1955), and Michael Conzen's echo *The Making of the American Landscape* (Unwin Hyman: Boston, Mass., 1990) ignore the cultural representation of landscape – for which both are the poorer.

2. See *The World Landscapes* series edited by J. M. Houston (Longmans: London, 1982–3).

3. Michael Williams, *Americans and their Forest: A Historical Geography* (Cambridge UP: Cambridge, 1989).

4. For a recent introduction to this debate, see Paul Giles, 'Reconstructing American Studies: Transnational Paradoxes, Comparative Perspectives', *Journal of American Studies* 28 (1994), no. 3, pp. 335–58.

5. J. B. Jackson maintains that landscape is but part of what surrounds us, being 'not a scenic or ecological entity but ... a political or cultural entity, changing in the course of history': 'The Order of a Landscape: Reason and Religion in Newtonian America', in D. W. Meinig (ed.), *The Interpretation of Ordinary Landscapes* (Oxford UP: New York, 1979), pp. 153–63.

6. Ralph Hyde, *Panoramania! The Art and Entertainment of the 'All-Embracing' View* (Trefoil: London, 1988), and Jonathan Bayer, *The Panoramic Image* (John Hansard Gallery: Southampton, 1981). For a specifically US view, see John L. Marsh, 'Drama and Spectacle by the Yard: The Panorama in America', *Journal of Popular Culture* 10/3 (Winter 1976), pp. 581–92.

7. This introduction was written after reading Jay Appleton, *The Experience of Landscape* (John Wiley: London, 1975).

8. For further details of American physical environments, particularly the debate over how human or undisturbed the landscape was upon the arrival of the Europeans, see 'Suggestions for further reading'.

9. The best-known example of this approach is probably Carl Sauer's 'The Morphology of Landscape' (1926): see John Leighly (ed.), *Land and Life: A Selection from the Writings of Carl Ortwin Sauer* (University of California Press: Berkeley, 1963).

10. Terry G. Jordan, *Texas Log Buildings: A Folk Architecture* (University of Texas Press: Austin, 1978), or *Texas Graveyards: A Cultural Legacy* (University of Texas Press: Austin, 1982). The titles alone suggest the flavour of this approach.

11. Joseph S. Wood, ' "Build, Therefore, Your Own World": The New England Village as Settlement Ideal', *Annals of the Association of American Geographers* 81 (1991), pp. 32–50, is a most useful summary, critique and bibliographical source for this topic.

12. For a useful introduction, see the 'Amish' essay by John A. Hostetler in Stephan Thernstrom (ed.), *Harvard Enclycopedia of American Ethnic Groups* (Harvard UP: Cambridge, Mass., 1980), pp. 122–5.

13. Sam B. Hilliard, 'Plantations and the Moulding of the Southern Landscape', in Conzen (ed.), *The Making of the American Landscape*, pp. 104–26.

14. Yi-Fu Tuan, 'Geography, Phenomenology and the Study of Human Nature', *Canadian Geographer* 15/3 (1971), pp. 181–92.

CHAPTER I

The Physical Environment

Before the arrival of the first people, there was, of course, a fully developed yet ever-changing geography of those lands that would one day become the United States of America. Regional diversity existed, a product of that complex and ongoing interplay between the topography, the climate, and the consequent natural flora and fauna. Since each of these elements continues to exert a considerable influence on the range of landscape impact, it is worth recalling them in turn.

The topography of the United States is actually quite simple in outline. The lie of the land is essentially north–south, with two great mountain ranges: the Appalachians in the east; the Rockies in the west. Between them lies the great southwards-draining basin of the Mississippi-Missouri-Ohio lowlands. Unlike many equivalent Russian rivers, which drain northwards and so freeze at their outflow, these US rivers drain a vast area southwards into the ever-open Gulf of Mexico. In the past, great sheets of ice have moved southwards over this terrain, pushing soil before it, only to leave great mounds of rock, known as moraine, as the ice melted. Long Island in southern New York is probably the best-known example of this. Whereas most of Canada was ice-scoured, most of the USA lay either south of the invading ice sheets or in the zone of deposit, where soil pushed south was just dumped; when vegetation gradually took over the recently exposed lands that would later become the USA, there was the making of some of the richest, deepest soils in the world, upon which great forests and grasslands extended. The mountains of the east, the Appalachians, are geologically very old and, as such, have been considerably worn down over the ages. Even so, they stand over 2,000 metres high in the Great Smokies and, throughout their length from New England almost to the Gulf of Mexico, they act as a wide barrier to any passage between the Atlantic and the interior lowlands; being so high, they bring northern conditions deep into the southern states. To the west of the interior lowlands lie the Rocky Mountains, a younger and considerably higher range of mountains and plateaux which almost totally exclude Pacific influences from penetrating the interior lowlands. Part of a great mountain chain that stretches from Alaska in the north to the Andes in the south, the Rocky Mountains are a complex system, wide enough to encompass alpine-like peaks, pastures and glaciers, broad desert plateaux, and, along the Pacific coastal range, active volcanoes and earthquake zones, indicative of this area's role at the junction of the great Pacific and American tectonic plates.[1]

This physical structure acts as a huge barrier, keeping temperate ocean influences out of the interior lowlands, particularly in the eastern lee of the Rocky Mountains. However, air from the Arctic to the north and the Gulf of Mexico to the south has an almost untrammelled access deep into the continental interior. In winter, cold air can sweep south across almost the whole of the USA; conversely, in summer, hot and humid conditions reach up even into Canada. And when these rival air masses meet in conflict upon the plains, tornadoes can and do devastate wide areas of the country, as the film *Twister* (1996) has shown. Only the coastal areas along the Pacific escape the worst of these extremes. Even the Atlantic coastlands are inundated by either cold Arctic or hot Gulf air, often for weeks at a time, with the added factor of hurricanes, as great energy surges move off the hot southern waters to devastate the land where they come ashore.

The vastness of the USA has major implications for regional variation, so much a part of landscape variation even today: the larger the land mass, the greater the latitudinal and altitudinal variation, with all the consequent diversity of flora and fauna (and hence agricultural potential). Vastness on a continental scale enhances the potential for finding rare and strategic materials, but also increases the likelihood that certain types of ecological niches and, therefore, otherwise unlikely environments, such as deserts on the lee side of mountain ranges, will be present. As a major part of a continental land mass, the USA has not only a long geological history, but also a wider variety of landscape relics, such as the older Appalachians and the younger 'Alpine' Rockies, than is found in the UK. A continental scale does not only mean that there is a wide climatic variation, but that weather extremes are a major part of human experience, particularly on the high plains. But size alone does not distinguish the USA from Canada or Russia. It is the fact that the USA is mainly mid-latitude (the Alaskan and Hawaiian exceptions being but two of fifty states). It thus enjoys a greater variety of ecosystems than either rival, with fewer Arctic problems. On the other hand, unlike Brazil, for instance, the USA has comparatively small subtropical areas, and those that it does have, as in California and Florida, are useful adjuncts to a mostly temperate American heartland.

Landscapes of discovery

Before the arrival of people from across the Bering Strait, the landscapes of the New World were the unadulterated result of major physical processes, plus such comparatively minor modification as animals alone can induce. In the wide spread of geological time, mountains were raised up, eroded, and raised again; deserts waxed and waned; forests shifted; species changed. This whole tapestry evolved – a journey bound for nowhere in particular – until, that is, people arrived. Early arrivals from Asia soon sought to modify both where they lived and where they hunted. Indeed, one of the most remarkable recent discoveries has been the widespread impact of such early, supposedly primitive, human activity.[2] As populations moved to keep ahead of the great ice sheets – following the migrating herds from which so many took their food – fire, in particular, was a vital feature of human habitation. Over many generations, the use of fire in the hunt seems to have had a significant impact upon the way in which grasslands expanded at the expense of the forests. When the first Europeans arrived from across the Atlantic, therefore, they discovered not a pristine natural world, but a human landscape, though one created by people whose humanity they so often failed to recognise.[3] It was hardly surprising that, for many generations, these newcomers believed, paradoxically, that they alone could alter the landscape. And yet, initially at least, these settlers left scant trace, except locally around their fragile beachheads. However, the example of both the native peoples and of the early European colonists indicates that it is almost impossible to consider the creation of landscapes without regard for the way in which people viewed themselves and their role within their surroundings.

It has long been conventional to open any discussion of the US landscape with considerably more coverage of its physical environments than is provided here, but, for those of us concerned with the USA as a human society and not just as a slice of real estate, our continuing focus should be the human experience of this topography rather than the physical geography for its own sake.[4] A physical environment that is merely catalogued, mapped and surveyed remains foreign to most people's experience, even today. It is just not the way that people respond to their surroundings. Such an alienating 'scientific' attitude towards the world was almost unknown to earlier generations. The notable exception, perhaps, was Thomas Jefferson, who, in his *Notes on the State of Virginia* (1784), set the tone for many a subsequent geography-cum-encyclopaedia. A mass of barely undifferentiated data, with lists of mountains from various eras, glacial stages and their landscape traces, followed by a catalogue of flora and fauna with their geographical extent, seems, at best, antiquarian today. For early arrivals in the Americas, it was their *image* of the landscape that was real – real, in that it was their image of the surroundings rather than the surroundings themselves which coloured what they experienced. For the conquistador, the image of great cities full of gold was far more real than mere distractions such as drought and dust. A more realistic evaluation of the hazards involved in subduing a continent would probably have stopped Cortés dead in his tracks. Latter-day pilgrims such as the Mormon followers of Brigham Young could see a landscape of promise in the view from the Wasatch Mountains, a new promised land for a new chosen people, rather than the salt desert it was. Indeed, modern psychologists suggest that people react to their surroundings in terms of a mental map of what is expected rather than in terms of what is actually there.[5] Settlers usually had very little accurate or reliable information about the New World. They operated within an array of images that reflected their perception of that world, images which were frequently landscape-based. Here was to be a land flowing with milk and honey, a new Arcadia. It is not just today's arrivals who set foot upon a shore with which they feel, initially at least, deeply familiar.

The earliest explorers were seeking access to the riches of the Indies. When people realised that they had stumbled upon a new continent, however, there was already a long history of what to expect beyond the setting sun. Fishermen's tales from the Grand Banks of the North-west Atlantic became entangled with the tales of mystical lands of perfect peace, whether Utopia or Atlantis. Beyond the sunset lay a better world, or, at the very least, riches. One recurrent aspect of these images was of Arcadia, a place where a lost golden age could be rediscovered. Initial reportings of native peoples living amidst subtropical plenty confirmed the discovery of a place where the European scourge of scarcity could be left behind. Here a golden age could surely dawn. When the Italian Verrazano reported that the mouth of the Chesapeake was lush and verdant, Europeans recalled the landscapes of classical times. Here was Virgil's Arcadia, fecund and abundant. Illustrations from those early explorations present landscapes of nubile goddesses amidst rural plenty, lush vegetation and exotic fruits. Tame fauna, such as wild turkeys, ensured that no one would go hungry. The fish practically leapt out onto the river bank, and fowl begged hunters to shoot them out of the sky. While such images were deeply compromised by their role in promoting settlement, they do provide a glimpse of what so many Europeans wanted to see: a landscape fit for a new start, whether for themselves individually or within a community.

Reality, of course, rarely confirmed this imagined Utopia. Forests, swamps, savage wild animals and unexpectedly violent climatic extremes suggested wilderness rather than Arcadia. Sometimes the native peoples resisted rather than welcomed incomers, and, if the land was fertile, it had to be cleared first. Few settlers, except perhaps the Ulster Scots ('Scotch-Irish'), had survival strategies geared to frontier realities. Images of a wilderness came to dominate settlers' reports, especially amongst the Puritan communities attempting to carve out a New England. Potential there might be, but hard work and eternal vigilance were ever necessary for survival. Even the Pilgrim Fathers recorded that 'the whole countrie, full of woods and thickets, represented a wild and savage hiew'.[6] It soon became apparent that settlers had swapped a decadent homeland for one of ever-encroaching wilderness. This probably suited the Puritan communities, with their views on the threatening nature of the world, rather better than a landscape of welcoming prosperity would have done. Here on a barren shore they could envisage themselves as another tribe of Israel, searching out a promised land amidst a harsh and threatening world – as, two hundred years later, the Mormons were to do far inland.

Whether in communitarian New England or in the more individualistic southern colonies, the wilderness was there to be cut back. Techniques from Europe that had been geared to maintaining and extending long-settled landscapes had to be transformed into techniques for survival in hostile wilderness conditions. It was a colonial commonplace that what had worked in the Old Country would not necessarily work in America. The theodolite, for instance, was seen as being more appropriate for the settled lands of Europe.[7] In a primeval forested New World, other techniques would be required: 'Everywhere [is] covered with woods ... Here are no churches, Towers, Houses or peaked

Mountains to be seen from afar, no means of obtaining the Bearings or Distances of Places, but by the Compass, and actual Mensuration with the Chain.'[8]

Out of almost primeval forests and grasslands, generations of settlers created their own rural landscapes, combining half-remembered elements from Europe with American resources to create a westward spread of individual farmsteads, fields, fences and barns. The difficulties of westward expansion encouraged settlers to borrow techniques from ethnically distinct neighbours.[9] German carpentry techniques appear in Ulster Scots barns almost as soon as Indian corn turned up in settler diets. Those who refused such pragmatic adjustments stood a good chance of succumbing to the winter's storms, or of being vulnerable when native peoples fought back. Such frontier settlements, cut hurriedly out of wilderness conditions, seemed primitive even when they were materially comfortable, especially to visitors from the Old World, who often delighted in reporting back how rude and uncouth this New World really was. In her classic *Domestic Manners of the Americans* (1832), Mrs Trollope [10] could hardly contain her disgust at frontier Ohio, where, even in the 1830s, Americans' dwellings were as rude as their democratic behaviour. Mrs Trollope had expected to find not a wilderness, but a Utopia, or at least the beginnings of such, at the Nashoba community above Memphis. The reality of the wilderness quickly ended all such expectations. She could hardly leave fast enough. Idealism melted in the face of frontier practicalities. From afar, America was Arcadia; on the ground, it was a desolate wilderness, as Dickens was to remind British readers in *Martin Chuzzlewit* (1844).

New arrivals' expectations about the west have long been problematic. Explorers and settlers arrived not just from different directions, having experience of very different environments, but with very different mental maps of what was to be anticipated. The extent of geographical knowledge varied considerably. Initially, the only outsiders with any first-hand experience of even the southern plains were the Spanish pushing northwards. The first British penetration came south from the lands of the Hudson's Bay Company. Seeking to encourage hunting and the fur trade, grasslands were labelled 'barrens', unlike the sought-after aspen forest. Though French from the east seem to have acquired considerably more understanding of the grasslands from their more sustained contact with native peoples, these quite separate imperial images were not widely exchanged, inhibiting any comprehensive understanding of the region's unique set of environments. Even official reports could be misunderstood. Terms like 'barrens', which were never clearly defined, were open to misinterpretation. Arriving Americans also considered this area distinct, in that it was inadequately mapped and seemed to have little value for the fur trade. By the early nineteenth century, a synthesis of previous evaluations was emerging, as individual traders came to move between the different imperial domains, though the overall message remained one of desert, an image seemingly sustained by various more overtly scientific US expeditions. The Lewis and Clark expedition, sent westwards in 1804 beyond the Louisiana Purchase, newly acquired by President Jefferson, set a precedent for many such official forays into the Far West throughout the century. Pike's trek down the Santa Fé trail between 1806 and 1813 claimed that the Great Plains were uninhabitable, and Long's Yellowstone expedition in 1819–20 reported them 'almost wholly unfit for cultivation ... uninhabitable by a people depending upon agriculture'.[11] Forest gave way to 'barrens', beyond which lay an area labelled on the expedition map as the 'Great American Desert'. So the avowedly scientific nature of these initiatives did not challenge the reproduction of what were often quite complex, ambivalent or even misleading environmental images. Here the Garden of Eden finally seemed to give out. Rivers were shallow, muddy and intermittent. The grass was thin and short. Images of fertility and abundance ebbed away. Beyond the forest, the big sky was threateningly vast, the summers as long and harsh as the winters were cold and windswept.

Had it not been for the governmental promotion of a promised land even further west, in the Columbia Basin (plus the lure of Californian gold), settlement might well have come to a halt at the break of the plains. Competition in the 1860s between various routes for the proposed transcontinental railroad link compounded misleading images of much of this area in a wealth of descriptions used to promote or deter settlement. The 'Great American Desert' label was further 'confirmed' by off-putting references to sagebrush and cactus rather than accurate grassland images. The High Plains became negatively stereotyped not just within the USA, but overseas, and they were avoided by new arrivals in favour of lands far across the mountains. An official UK report concluded:

> The fertile savannas and valuable woodlands of the Atlantic United
> States are succeeded on the West by more or less arid desert,

occupying a region on both sides of the Rockies, which creates a barrier to the continuous growth of settlements between the Mississippi Valley and the states on the Pacific coast.[12]

Such images portrayed the high plains as an inert frontier, encouraging settlers to consider the Pacific coastlands instead, which suited US strategic needs to fill their newly acquired territories in the Far West.

Frontier studies periodically debate the influence, if any, of this pejorative labelling of the high plains as the Great American Desert. Some maintain that this label was quite sufficient to explain the leap-frogging by both government and settlers to more obviously fertile lands further west. Only sustained and sanctioned environmental prejudice could account for the re-establishment of the 'hollow frontier' of the colonial era, quite at odds with Jefferson's notions of an organised, compact line of settlement as inaugurated in the Ohio lands of the 1790s. Others maintain that settlers had forgotten this 'desert' label by the end of the century, albeit to their cost, due to the unusual run of moist years; this led to disaster when normal desert conditions, the Dust Bowl, re-established themselves. Still others have argued that 'desert' never meant hot and dry at all, only deserted, which it obviously was, but not necessarily for reasons of drought.[13]

For many settlers from the east, treelessness was proof of the soil's inherent infertility. Coming from a wood-based culture, settlers required vast amounts of cheap timber for fuel, building materials, fencing and farm implements. Popular aversion to the plains may, however, say as much about the needs of later generations for certain levels of capital investment and technological improvements (deep ploughs, barbed wire and cheap wind pumps), along with an unprecedented demand for cheap food, than about any bucolic idiocy peculiar to the first settlers. On the plains, the prairie bison were replaced by longhorn cattle for shipment eastwards. As eastern markets for food grew apace, and the transcontinental railroads criss-crossed the prairie lands, the 'sod-busting' farmers ploughed up the virgin grasslands, driving the cattle barons into the hills or into urban feedlots. Free or cheap land, an unusually moist few decades after initial settlement, coupled with factory farming techniques, meant that the acreage rose, productivity climbed and profitability was enhanced, until it collapsed in the over-cropping, monoculture of the 1920s, exposing the area's ecological fragility. At last human endeavour had created a truly Great American

Desert, whose memory still haunts the plains. Though New Deal county agents promoted contour ploughing, wind-breaks, the damming of gullied creeks, plus the advantage of leaving fields fallow for many years to minimise erosion and dust-blows, later erosion and thinning soils suggest that the environmental lessons of the 1930s may have been ignored in the face of debts and foreclosures, acreage increases, and dependence upon volatile foreign markets (such as the former USSR). By the 1990s, some farmers seriously considered returning the High Plains to the buffalo. Landscapes equivalent to those of 1492 may yet emerge, just as forest has returned to the Appalachians. But the plains will never be quite the same. The identification of past landscapes and the recognition of their place in the evolution of present landscapes is far from being an antiquarian pursuit. And the influence of these present representations of images, superimposed upon relics of past landscapes within the constraints of modern farming, ensures that landscape analysis can be both complex and problematic.

Wide ecological variation is part of the USA's rich tapestry of landscape variation, but the way in which people responded to this variation depended upon their varying avenues of approach, the 'cultural baggage' with which they experienced and made sense of the variation, as well as the impact of their technology. British groups based along the Atlantic first experienced the considerable temperate (yet, to them, seemingly humid) latitudinal variation in terms of its contrasts with the Old Country. Measured against their folk memories and the idealised claims of promoters and sponsors alike, the New World was often found wanting. In many instances, they responded by carving up the wilderness into suitably tamed, 'English' vistas – or at least pretended, with their familiar fireplaces and furniture, that the outside world was less strange than they actually found it to be. It took many generations for American conditions to be recognised as normal. Ironically, by the early nineteenth century these Tidewater conditions had become the benchmark against which further inland conditions were to be measured: the landscape norm had shifted from Europe to the Atlantic coast. East coast landscapes extended into the interior as New Englanders moved across New York into the Ohio country. In the south, plantation society pushed aside the Civilized Tribes to spread westwards to the Mississippi and beyond.[14] Only when cotton reached certain climatic limits just before the Civil War, did settlers come to reconsider the universal utility of their livelihood and its associated landscapes.

Further north, the landscapes created by the Northwest Ordinance in the late eighteenth century assumed that all soils at this latitude would have high fertility levels. Here was a landscape suitable for the humid east, applied ever westwards irrespective of changing ecological conditions. Unfortunately, this westward transition of a humid forested landscape into one of savannah lands and, finally, desert margins was so gradual that few felt the need to re-evaluate their settlement techniques. And, arriving within one of the moistest thirty-year spells in modern history, settlers saw what they wanted to see – a potential garden, given enough hard work. Political pressure to reduce the sizes of lots rather than increase them, so that settlers could afford to buy land directly from the government, reached its culmination in the Homestead Act of 1862. However democratically worthy and strategically necessary, the landscape impact of this measure was to be dramatic. With ever more technologically advanced equipment, farmers were able to secure ever better crop yields off ever smaller farms. When economic dislocation compounded agricultural decline in the years following the First World War, a dust bowl lay exposed, a landscape of personal and ecological disaster.[15]

The more informed agricultural programmes of the New Deal stemmed this tide of dust and ecological collapse. Subsequent agricultural prosperity has helped to both sustain the US standard of living and to provide surplus foodstuffs for export. However, all this has been achieved at a growing cost, increasingly visible on the contemporary landscape. Farmsteads are merged and, as in the 1930s, buildings are pulled down, left to rot, or reused for domestic purposes. Corporate farms amalgamate under the changing pattern of crops, irrigation and increased mechanisation. New crop strains consolidate a landscape geared to agri-business, a far cry from the Jeffersonian aspirations of the 1780s, while the pressure to sell land near cities for golf courses, colleges, or just for residential development becomes ever more powerful. Few farmers can resist the developer's siren call to pay off all those debts, put the kids through college, and retire to Florida on the proceeds!

Little of the original flora and fauna remains as it was in 1492, even in the forested parts of Appalachia. The modern forest cover is almost all regrowth, often either converted to waste, as with the strip-mined areas of central Appalachia, or disturbed to make way for ski resorts or other leisure attractions, including theme parks. All the wild landscapes, at least in the east, have been tamed, each in its own way. Only in restricted reserves, along with certain watercourses, and in wind-breaks can traces of the original flora and fauna be found. In the west, the situation initially seems substantially different. But closer scrutiny suggests otherwise. Much of the wilderness in Alaska is being maintained by conscious public designation, yet even these areas are open to exploitation when pressures reach critical levels. The North Slope, for example, has become a major oil producer; south, to the open sea, the mountain ranges are now crossed by oil pipelines, access roads, and the gradually encroaching provision of resort facilities. Even those areas not so affected have military installations, tracking facilities, and scientific research bases. In the western lands of the lower forty-eight states, pristine deserts are now crossed by interstate highways, natural wonders such as the Grand Canyon are surrounded by resorts, and even the giant redwoods are scientifically managed. There is really very little that has survived from the first substantial arrival of Europeans in 1492. The landscapes that they found are now recognised to be human rather than natural, landscapes reflecting the indigenous peoples' long and stable accommodation across a wide array of ecological niches. Europeans were to shatter these long-standing relationships; with ever-growing populations and desire to exploit their new surroundings, the landscape would be changed for ever.

Notes

1. Stanley W. Trimble, 'Nature's Continent', pp. 9-26. Michael Conzen (ed.), *The Making of the American Landscape* (Unwin Hyman: Boston, Mass., 1990), provides a useful overview. More detail can be found in Ron Redfern, *The Making of a Continent* (BBC: London, 1983).

2. See Louis de Vorsey, 'The New Land: The Discovery and Exploration of the Eastern North America', in Robert D. Mitchell and Paul A. Groves (eds), *North America* (Hutchinson: London, 1987), pp. 25–47.

3. See Karl W. Butzer, 'The Indian Legacy in the American Landscape', in Conzen (ed.), *The Making of the American Landscape*, pp. 27–50.

4. For a novel introduction to US physical variety as experienced by settlers see Robert Peck, *The Land of the Eagle* (BBC: London, 1989). For a more biotic focus, see also *Bellamy's New World: A Botanical History of America* (BBC: London, 1983).

5. Peter Gould and Rodney White, 'The Images of Places', in *Mental Maps* (Penguin: Harmondsworth, 1974), pp. 15–49.

6. William Bradford, 1620, as quoted by Leo Marx, *The Machine in the Garden* (Oxford University Press: New York, 1964), p. 41.

7. Brian Friel's play *Translations* (Faber and Faber: London, 1981), explores subversive responses to British colonial surveying techniques dependent upon the theodolite.

8. Notes to accompany the *General Map of the Middle Colonies in America*, published

in 1755 and discussed in Simon Berthon and Andrew Robinson, *The Shape of the World: The Mapping and Discovery of the East* (George Philip: London, 1991), p. 152.

9. See the discussion over the supposedly Finnish origins of the frontier log cabin in Terry G. Jordan and Matti Kaups, *The American Backwoods Frontier, an Ethnic and Ecological Interpretation* (The Johns Hopkins Press: Baltimore, 1981). Copenhagen's Fridlandsmuseet has examples of pre-emigration cabins in re-created surroundings, while Omagh's Ulster American Folk Park displays post-emigration examples in its reconstructed frontier settlement.

10. Frances Trollope, *The Domestic Manners of the Americans* (1832) (Sutton: Gloucester, 1984).

11. Clyde A. Milner, II, *Major Problems in the History of the American West* (D.C. Heath: Lexington, Mass., 1989), p. 141. See also Martyn J. Bowden, 'The Great American Desert in the American mind', in David Lowenthal and Martyn J. Bowden, *Geographies of the Mind* (Oxford UP: New York, 1976), pp. 119–47.

12. J. Passiser, *Journals, Detailed Reports and Observations* (HMSO: London, 1863).

13. A useful summary of this issue can be found in D. A. Brown's review of Merlin P. Lawson, *The Climate of the Great American Desert* (University of Nebraska Press: Lincoln, 1974), in *Annals of the Association of American Geography* 67 (1977), pp. 606–8.

14. Grant Foreman, *Indian Removal: The Emigration of the Five Civilized Tribes* (Norman: Oklahoma, 1932).

15. There is a wide literature on ecological collapse in the 1930s. For a useful summary, see Donald Worster, *Dust Bowl* (Oxford University Press: New York, 1979).

CHAPTER 2

Cultural Landscapes:
The Imperial Legacy

The modern United States of America covers territory far wider and
more diverse than those areas of the British Empire that gained their
independence in the 1780s. The Great Lakes and the Ohio and Mississippi valleys were once part of a French Empire that stretched from the
St Lawrence to the Gulf of Mexico. Further west lay the northern reaches
of New Spain, while to the north-west the Russians continued their
colonisation of Siberia eastwards into Alaska and southwards along the
coast to California. Where possible, the imperial powers ignored the
native peoples, their societies and their political institutions, subduing
all by a variety of military, diplomatic or economic strategies. Little
remains in the contemporary landscape of these 'First Nations' (as they
are called today in Canada), except locally in the reservations of the Far
West and in place-names such as Massachusetts and the Dakotas. The
legacies of France, Russia and Spain also seem equally fragile at times,
except again locally. Russian churches and place-names can be found
along the Pacific north-west (though Alaska's position, isolated from
the other states, is probably the most secure legacy of Russia colonisation).[1] Throughout much of the Midwest, French influences are few and
far between, buried in Americanised pronunciations of such places as
Detroit and St Louis,[2] quite unlike the vibrant French-speaking society
of Quebec to the north, in Canada. Only in southern Louisiana, with
its rural Cajun and urban Creole populations, has French culture retained
sufficient hold on the pulse of life to create and sustain a distinct cultural
landscape.[3] Most widely known for its locally distinct race relations,
music and cuisine, it is no less evident in the rural landscape, where
long lots reaching back from the waterfront access into the bayou
country create a landscape that echoes that of Quebec rather than the
rectangular survey of so much of the American west.

Whereas native and French influences upon the contemporary landscape are either difficult to ascertain or are isolated in certain localised

areas, the influence of Spain is more significant.[4] Although the present south-western states occupy territory that was at the very margins of Spanish power in the New World, the legacy of Spain – or, at least, Mexico – is everywhere,[5] exemplified in such familiar names as Los Angeles or San Francisco and by the legacy of Spanish land claims on the layout of many farmlands.[6] While much of this Spanish influence has been swamped by the influx of Anglo-Americans, what has not been eliminated is the area's proximity to Mexico, whose people for generations have crossed the border as if it did not exist to seek casual work in the fields or to stay and raise their children within a society whose wealth they could never hope to enjoy back home. Unlike the immigrants who entered the New World in the last century, however, these people do not make an equivalent journey to the long Atlantic voyage. Hope may lie north of the border for them, but social and family links are not severed, as they were for Poles and Jews. Thus Los Angeles is becoming a major Spanish-speaking city whose air waves and billboards are full of a vibrant and increasingly self-confident Spanish. A uniquely sustainable non-White Anglo-Saxon Protestant society is being created here which challenges WASP notions of what the USA is to be. And the impact of this process is increasingly evident not just on the landscape, but in the political process, which may eventually change the very nature of American society.[7]

But what of the British imperial legacy to the contemporary US landscape? In the east, the legacy is evident in many overt ways, for it was along the Atlantic coast that a variety of British offshoot societies first became established. Further west, the legacy is more subtle, but no less important. None of the original colonies was a complete replica of even one aspect of the home country.[8] New England, the northern colonies, were by and large theocratic, restraining – or at least harnessing – individualism to the greater glory of God and the community.[9] Overwhelmingly English in character, settlers created a landscape that was uniquely their own even while echoing certain English traits. Whatever the historical reality contained in the popular image of the New England village, its white spire church and village green, there can be no doubt that these societies were important in feeding a particular sense of community into the Midwest as New Englanders moved to the frontier after independence.[10] In the Mormon creations of nineteenth-century Utah, for example, can be seen the Puritan legacy, a landscape of prosperity dedicated to the glory of God, living proof of salvation, and a challenge to other notions of American individualism to be found outside New England and its offshoots.[11] For the Puritans were not the only religious groups to settle in the English colonies. Quakers forged out a more liberal, certainly a more heterogeneous, commonwealth west of the Delaware River. By encouraging the settlement of Protestant sects fleeing oppression in Europe, Pennsylvania became home to Welsh Quakers,[12] Ulster Presbyterians,[13] German Mennonites,[14] the Amish of Lancaster County [15] and beyond, all of whom took rival notions of individualism and community into the mountain frontier to create landscapes quite different from those of New England. And further south still, a range of entrepreneurial but no less religiously minded colonies were founded that sought to create yet another New World along the Chesapeake and then, afterwards, inland. Based upon the export of staple raw materials to Britain, these southern colonies came increasingly to depend not just upon large estates worked by tenants or landless labourers and upon a plethora of small farmers who hoped, through hard work and careful trading, to expand their holdings and their standing within society, but also upon indentured servants and, most significantly, growing numbers of African slaves. Despite the extensive contribution of small farms to westward expansion, it was the growth of these increasingly slave-based plantations [16] that came to dominate the distinctiveness of this region as a cultural landscape. The hollow frontier, where settlers moved not to an immediately adjacent piece of land, but to a further isolated patch, leaving the intervening territory for late arrivals, became a classic element of this southern frontier landscape which, in the ante-bellum period, spread across the land of the Civilized Tribes westwards to the Mississippi and beyond into eastern Texas. As the Ohio country filled with free labour, increasingly from overseas, the contrast between these southern lands and what later generations would call the 'Midwest' became ever more apparent, especially when settlers from both traditions came to live in the same parts of the Louisiana Purchase, such as Kansas and Nebraska. Only when southern settlers moved into the northern reaches of Mexico did the resulting cultural landscape change significantly, incorporating those Spanish traditions and land uses which could not be eliminated. Even today, Texas is both a place apart and yet still a western extension of the south, whose side it took in the 'War between the States'.[17]

It is common to see western landscapes as emerging as quite distinct from those of the east. But the western rectangular landscape was first experienced east of the Mississippi, within the first US territory to be developed, the Northwest Territory, lying between the Great Lakes and the Ohio River. Furthermore, this seemingly revolutionary new landscape did not appear from nowhere. Precedents clearly existed east of the Appalachians, within the Atlantic coast settlements. Indeed, if one person is to claim authorship of the western lands, it must surely be Thomas Jefferson. Although Jefferson did not seek merely to replicate the landscape of his native state in the west, it was within Virginia that he developed his ideas. Thus it is as well to appreciate something of Virginia's early landscape evolution before moving on to explore Jefferson's great landscape creation in the Ohio country, the Northwest Territory.

Virginia: the creation of an American landscape

No single state can encompass the environmental variation of America's east coast, not even one that extends from the Atlantic to the Cumberland Gap across the Appalachians. It was within Virginia's wide range of environments, however, that the first permanent English colony was to be sited in the early seventeenth century. From their toe-hold on the James River, settlers gradually moved upstream to explore an already human landscape. Unable to read the landscape as they had at home, these early settlers made many, often elementary, mistakes, overworking unsuitable land while ignoring better areas. For many settlers, the landscape they sought was one of their own devising, a landscape tamed as only they knew how. Building techniques were initially those of the Old Country, though materials were increasingly novel and unpredictable. The interior landscapes of house and barn were re-created wherever possible, even where particular features such as large indoor fireplaces were not always advisable. But even where the public landscape came to resemble that of mother England, with its court-house and church, its gaol and pound, its open commons and enclosed fields, the detail of the Virginia landscape came to assume its own peculiar form. The fields held tobacco for export. The hard manual labour at the brickyard, on the wharf, or in the field was increasingly that of Africans held captive in perpetuity. Though an English pedigree remained sharply defined, the increasingly local character of these Virginia settlements came ever to the fore. And as the plantation way of life, with its own distinctive economic and cultural landscape, moved inland, away from the Tidewater, the image of Virginia as one of wilderness gradually gave way to one of verdant prosperity, to be protected as much from British imperial interference without as from the native peoples, African slaves, and the growing number of small farmers within.[18]

But just as the landscapes of the Tidewater started to extend into the rolling hills of the more isolated Piedmont, so colonists from the north, beyond the Potomac, started to arrive inland, driving a cultural wedge into Virginia life that was always to show itself within the life and landscape of the Old Dominion. German and Ulster-Scots settlers from Penn's Quaker commonwealth, with few links to Tidewater life, found their way south-westwards, over the Maryland panhandle, into the Great Valley of the Shenandoah, then the far reaches of Virginia's frontier.[19] Seeking affordable land, these settlers entered Virginia by a back door, one that must have seemed unguarded and unclaimed. There was scant trace of any human settlement, Indian no less than European, with little if any sign of Virginia's sovereignty. For established Virginia society, based around Tidewater Williamsburg, this frontier influx was a mixed blessing. Though holding the frontier, these newcomers felt scant loyalty towards the distant, Tidewater-based political system. Religious affiliation, family loyalty and existing commercial ties lay down the Great Valley, to family and friends in Maryland and Pennsylvania, not across the Blue Ridge and the Piedmont to the Chesapeake settlements. The very emptiness of the valley seemed to prove that these chosen people had entered their own chosen land, though the valley was probably uninhabited for reasons that were rooted in the religious life of the native peoples.

To Virginia's new frontier farmers, the Great Valley seemed like a God-given escape route from high land prices above the Potomac. Whether or not the various ethnic groups survived as recognisably distinct communities, with their own cultural landscapes, remains debatable, though Ulster families have been traced across much of the southern Appalachians.[20] Within Virginia itself, the contemporary landscape still reflects the historically created divide between the Tidewater-based plantation legacy of the lands east of the Blue Ridge and the mountain lands to the west.[21] So colonial Virginia, though archetypally southern in terms of race relations and the role of the plantation economy, also contained within it a major non-southern component, increasingly transplanted from further north. This, then, was the Virginia of Thomas Jefferson's own experience.

The Jeffersonian landscape

Thomas Jefferson chose to live in the Virginia Piedmont rather than in the plantation communities around the capital, Williamsburg. As a young man, he had explored the Great Valley frontier as settlers from Pennsylvania were arriving. He looked west, and had no desire to transplant the Virginia Tidewater across the new and expanding western lands.

And land there certainly was in the Americas, land for the taking. But how was the west to be transformed from a wilderness to a Garden of Eden suitable for a new republic? Access to such a bounty would fulfil Europeans' long-held dream for land. And land would make a true republic of yeoman farmers possible. America could become 'the land of the free' not just in terms of political experiments, involving best-practice constitutions, but in terms of spatial layouts that would suit popularly based administration and land allocation. Land was to be made available not just for the favoured few, the grand proprietors such as Penn or Oglethorpe, but for all those families wishing to work the land.

The family farm was to be considered a central feature of the republican countryside. If the Midwest today is still seen as representing perhaps the most all-American of regions, part of the reason for this lies not just in a dialect noticeably lacking the distinctive regionalisms of New England or the South, but in the uniformity of its settlement pattern. This stands in contrast to the more European, more higgledy-piggledy patchwork of Atlantic areas, particularly in Tidewater Virginia. The Midwest 'farmscape' appears American not just in its family-farm regularity, but in its lack of Old World complexity, a simplicity appropriate for a more egalitarian and homogenous republican society.[22] The surface of the land almost conspired with the imposition of the rational surveyed layout, so flat is it for hundreds of miles in almost every direction. With the arrival of American surveyors, the landscape of the Northwest Territory was changed completely. Previous European inroads into the Ohio country had been more transitory, voyageurs after pelts, traders after markets, and soldiers in defence of their imperial frontiers. But landscape changes had been localised around rendezvous sites, forest tracks ('traces') and forts. In Jefferson's imagination, the farmer would transform this utterly. The log cabin standing alone in the clearing or amidst the vastness of the prairie became a major image of the landscape of Jeffersonian self-sufficiency.[23]

Jefferson had a range of precedents in his consideration of a strategy for settling the western lands. The New England townships were communally based, with frontier expansion on a group rather than an individual basis. Southern communities had moved west in a far more dynamic manner, producing not just a hollow frontier, but a legacy of unresolved land-ownership lawsuits which inhibited rational economic development. Both these rival societies and their associated landscape were deemed increasingly inappropriate as a model of republican expansion into the interior. The individualism of the South, combined with the order of New England, was acceptable, but not slavery or group control. The landscape of the Northwest Territory was to be primarily a restatement of American values, rejecting those parts of the colonial experience deemed inappropriate for an expanding republican experiment. Thus the Founding Fathers had views on settlement options as they did on appropriate systems of government. In both cases, they sought to choose the best from the colonial past, to learn from the classical past, and to combine these elements in a form that would be both peculiarly American and universal in its future application.

Thomas Jefferson's Northwest Land Ordinance was designed to forge a truly republican and westward-looking USA. The new republic should avoid repeating both European feudalism and the urban-based capitalism that was replacing it. Being self-sufficient, the new agrarian nation would have no need for cities and all their attendant perils; it would not so much wipe out trade as make it unnecessary, confining the exchange of goods and services to local barter, with farmers dealing one with another on a mutual basis. The west should be surveyed and conveyanced to enhance self-sufficiency, therefore, with an administrative system that brought newly settled areas into full membership of the republic in due course. The peace treaty with Britain secured a free hand for US expansion to the Mississippi, its new western border. The sudden acquisition of this vast territory made a comprehensive land policy imperative if an unregulated land rush was not to lead to the kind of chaos which, detractors believed, would be an inevitable and fatal flaw in the democratic experiment. Chaos in western settlement could only encourage the return of the Loyalists, still smarting north of the Great Lakes, or even provoke an Indian uprising, which would stop all settlement dead in its tracks. It was vital to get the land-allocation system right and to create a system of government that retained frontier loyalties. Land was a central fact of American life, so land-allocation policies remained a central feature of US politics until at least the 1860s. Having abolished the last remnants of feudal ties (such as quit-rents and primogeniture), the new authorities set out to create a land policy appropriate for their ideal nation, one of individual and self-sufficient freeholders.

The French immigrant Crèvecoeur recognised that the American republic was 'not composed of great men who possess everything, and a herd of people who have nothing'. It was, rather, a nation of true producers of wealth, 'all tillers of the earth'. Yeomen, as farmers, were the republic's economic strength, as voters its political strength, and as good shots its military strength. As agriculturists working to effect Jefferson's aspirations, farmers were architects of a peculiarly American landscape. Crèvecoeur was enthusiastic about American agricultural prosperity as it already existed east of the Appalachians:

> Fair cities, substantial villages, extensive fields, an immense country filled with decent houses, good roads, orchards, meadows and bridges, where a hundred years ago all was wild, woody and uncultivated! What a train of pleasing ideas this spectacle must suggest; it is a prospect which must inspire a good citizen with the most heartfelt pleasure.[24]

It is this *settled* landscape that is most American, not the wilderness. It follows that the most American of peoples are those who create such a landscape from the wilderness. The farmer was thereby seen as a suitable *moral* basis for a republican society, as someone producing true wealth, rather than merely money. Producing food and shelter for family survival would, over the years, lead to a settled and productive landscape. Yeoman farmers were 'the chosen people of God' because, as Jefferson explained, 'corruption of morals in the mass of cultivators is a phenomenon of which no age nor nation has furnished an example'.[25] Land should be made so freely available as to exclude practically no one. There would be no landless tenants, for free land would always be available further west, making speculation in land inconceivable. Trade and manufacturing would be unthinkable, for 'the young American Republic, richly endowed with land, must be mated with the pure damsel of agriculture, commerce is a vixen and manufacturing a diseased harlot beside her'.[26]

With such words, Jefferson articulated American aspirations for the western lands; through chairing the governmental committee set up to organise their disposal, he came to put those aspirations into practice. Jefferson was arguably the major conduit through which dominant expectations were expressed and through whose plans such ideas were imposed upon the wilderness.

Central to western settlement would be the rejection of *ad hoc*, incremental expansion in favour of survey prior to settlement, with rectangular lots and townships that could be easily mapped and identified with link, chain and lines of sight. Lines of latitude and longitude would be used, reflecting the belief that human planning was most likely to succeed when in harmony with scientific principles. The now famous rectangular grid is essentially a visual construct imposed upon the land. Deep in the forest, with restricted lines of sight, a grid *per se* meant little; on a map, however, within a bill of sale, or, latterly, from a plane, it came into its own. When initially surveyed, an aerial perspective could only be imagined, of course. The western landscape had to be visualised before it could be developed. Indeed, congressmen were again and again to compare the western planning they were doing to effect a visual image that they already possessed. Even congressional debates had recourse to maps – or at least plans ('plats'). The west was, for them, as much a canvas as a focus for political experimentation.[27]

Jefferson's expectation was that land would be held fee-simple, that is, without any associated feudal obligation, unhampered by entail or restrictive covenants. It could thus be bought and sold freely, though the implication was that this would rarely happen. Land was primarily to be used, not exchanged; the republic would be as anti-capitalist as it was anti-feudal. From the very start, such expectations were unrealistic. The federal government had only been able to acquire the western lands from the states by offering to take over their revolutionary war debts. States could only be expected to relinquish their western collateral if, in so doing, they also disposed of their substantial liabilities. For the federal government to remain virtuous, as befitted a new republic, these debts had to be cleared as soon as possible by relinquishing the collateral. The six-mile square townships that had been surveyed in the Northwest Territory north of the Ohio River were offered for sale at auction, therefore, half as complete townships, half as individual lots. This immediately undermined, or at least opened up, this great experiment in self-sufficiency. Small farmers could not necessarily afford even the minimum lot made available; they would have to buy what they could afford from a middleman, who quickly bought up land for speculation. For years, frontier settlers sought to buy lots in sizes that they could afford direct from the public domain, rather than via a profit-taking middleman. But, in the main, farmers had to buy land and then develop it. Many found that, as they improved their land, neighbouring plots held by land companies rose in value, without their absentee owners lifting a finger. Farmers wishing to expand could not do so if the neighbouring land was held, awaiting a rise in property values, by absentee land companies, causing frustration which was often only re-solved by selling an improved lot to latecomers, thereby enabling the frontiersman to move further west to buy an even larger plot. Thus land came to be seen, by large and small owners alike, as a commodity to be bought and, perhaps, worked for its resale value. Improvements also cost money; farmers were soon producing not just for their own imme-diate needs, but for shipment elsewhere. As corn was too bulky to be shipped back east over the Appalachian Mountains, it would be fed to pigs which drovers would take to distant markets, along with rye or corn whiskey. Trade, commerce and industry duly emerged in the heart of the very landscape most geared to reflect and promote agrarian self-reliance. A market economy, rather than any non-feudal, non-capitalist third way, gradually and inexorably evolved as more and more of the west came under the sway of the growing commercial and increasingly industrial cities back east. When Mrs Trollope set up shop in Cincinnati in the late 1820s, this frontier town was already proud of its claim to be 'Hogopolis' to the world. To her dismay, pigs, slaughter-houses and offal seemed everywhere. A generation later, Chicago in its turn would be, in the poet Carl Sandberg's words, 'hog butcher to the world' – and proud of it.

The very use of an ordered, grid-based survey to allocate western land inaugurated a land-holding system geared to the buying and selling of land. Lots that had been surveyed and numbered prior to settlement were easy to find, delineate, convey and, finally, to sell. Profits from buying and selling land were available to promote both westward expansion *and* the emergence of a fully mature capitalist economy, following from, but antithetical to, Jeffersonian ideals. In a republic, land should be freely available to any citizen prepared to work it, engaging with his or her surroundings and neighbours in relation-ships that were not alienating, but meaningful and direct. Jefferson expected land to be a common heritage rather than a commodity for private sale.

Jefferson's landscape experiment confirmed that deterministic routes to social perfection are always flawed, if only by being hostage to fortune. It was not the relationship between settlers and the land that was crucial, but the basis of the relationship between settlers and outsiders. Once the principle of land as a commodity has been established, Jeffersonian ideals were no match for the subversive power of market forces. The legacy of the Jeffersonian ideal is not a self-sufficient agrarian republic, but a chequer-board landscape west from Ohio. By accident, the very format deemed most appropriate for a land of yeoman farmers turned out to be more suited to treating land as a commodity which could be labelled and pre-packaged. Like other raw materials, land could be bought and sold by those who had never even seen it. As a commodity, it had become as much a part of a futures market as any other resource, with each lot remaining more important for its potential than for its present productivity. The wilderness might seem impenetrable, but once neighbouring lots were developed, or a railway passed by, who knows what its worth might be. The eye might see half-burnt tree stumps and a shack, but the mind's eye could see fields of corn around a prosperous farmstead. The images of past landscapes, whether agrarian or patrician, might fire the eastern promoters of this exercise in social Utopia, but it was a vision of profitability, both commercial and entrepreneurial, that enveloped those who actually had to live within it. Many social revolutions leave, dotted across the landscape, elements now redundant, such as avenues of trees and monuments. The failed Jeffersonian revolution left such an impressive mark on the landscape precisely because its chequer-board landscape was so well suited to what followed – commercial agriculture based on capital investment, long-distance trading in commodities and the accumulation of ever larger blocks of land.

Jefferson, architect of the western territories, was also an architect at home. As he created rational western landscapes, so too he worked on creating a progressive variant of the degenerate Tidewater plantation on his Albemarle County estate. Here he applied classical notions imported from Europe not to enhance élitist visions, as had many humanist Europeans before him, but to serve as a context within which practical improvements and inventions could be promoted for utilitarian and democratic ends. Even as Jefferson looked forward, he nevertheless worked within the emerging landscape traditions of his class. Though he sought to enhance the productivity of his estate (and, ironically, it was not handed on as a financially going concern), Jefferson overtly set about creating a specific landscape – that is, one in which the visual aspect was a crucial consideration, not just the unintended product of economic activities. An overtly visual concern for landscape was not peculiar to Thomas Jefferson. The very word 'landscape' already had a long pedigree. It had initially appeared in English as 'landskip' in the late sixteenth century, a word and an image borrowed from the Dutch. Royal portraits had placed the patron against a suitable backdrop and so established the recurrent feature of English landscape painting up to Jefferson's time: the country house and its prospect.[28] The mood deemed suitable for such portraits was one of rural ease, productivity and abundance amidst the classical ideal of 'holy agriculture'. Such an estate would also represent the whole polity – an uncorrupted agrarian nation. This helped to generate an image of the ideal state that was to be expropriated by republicans such as Thomas Jefferson. In America, the new republican leaders would sustain their once English rights by promoting those rural virtues which agriculture alone keeps uncorrupted. Estate paintings are actually a crucial development in the Anglo-Saxon idea of landscape within which Thomas Jefferson lived and which, in his scholarly trips, he actively sought out and explored. Under the 'lordship' of the eye, all lies subordinate, as befits an overview of privately owned productive land. 'Looking forward' from a vantage point over an actual prospect, the writer or painter 'composes' it by arranging hills and dales, open champaigns and woodlands, light and shade, so that, in perspective, nature takes on the illusion of a picture, itself an illusion of nature constructed for the dissociated observer. The dual conversion of nature and art allows control over both.[29] The country-house picture makes the analogy between the well-run estate and the ruler's wider realm. Such pictures initially reinforced the ideology of landscape in the service of Stuart absolutism. American revolutionaries such as Thomas Jefferson learned this lesson well. Images of landscape were conjured up as appropriate for the political culture being promoted. He realised that the landscapes being built both locally and nationally should help to promote, or at least not hinder, the creation, promotion and success of America's democratic, land-based revolution. Each absolutist estate picture had presented the well-managed house and landscape as a microcosm of the wider, morally acceptable society, each estate a self-sufficient part of a self-sufficient whole. Thomas Jefferson sought to put such ideas into good effect on a wider canvas. A morally acceptable microcosm, a farm on its lot, would both represent and constitute an essential building block of an independent, self-sufficient New World, economically free as well as politically. Where the harmony of the absolutist estate rested upon the subordination of all to the landlord, a new landscape harmony would be created, appropriate to the needs of a post-revolutionary society. An ordered and pleasing prospect would only be possible in an ordered and democratic agrarian society. So Thomas Jefferson was as concerned with his country as with his estate, seeing the implications for each in the other.

How does Monticello compare with the English country house of the eighteenth century? Superficially, it is very similar: enclosed parkland around a country house. Monticello's neo-classical pedigree is more apparent here than in George Washington's Mount Vernon on the Potomac. When Renaissance Venice had sought to legitimate its imperial pretensions, the architect Palladio had turned to a pure Roman architectural style; in eighteenth-century England, this had become associated with the imagined moral and political perfection of republican Rome, a pristine era supposedly based upon agriculture and informal gardens. It was this English adaptation (or misreading) of the original source of Palladian ideas that was picked up by Americans. The builders' handbooks that did so much to help diffuse Palladianism were remarkably free of theoretical discussion. Once such practical approaches had arrived in America, they helped to promote classical styles of layout and ornamentation worthy and expressive of a republican nation.

The landscape of the new republic would solve the age-old problem of relating the aesthetic with the productive use of land. Whereas devices such as the ha-ha (or sunken ditch) had been used in Britain to allow cattle (or deer) to appear to be within the immediate vicinity of the house whilst nevertheless being kept safely at bay, no such manipulation of the prospect would be necessary in America. The productive was deemed aesthetically acceptable, a pre-echo, perhaps, of the 'form following function' maxim. All else was surely vanity. In contrast, when the new Palladian form became fashionable in Britain in the eighteenth century, the propertied classes had no qualms about removing whole, agriculturally viable, communities to 'enhance' the view. Upwardly mobile landlords had little interest in productive tenants who might stand in their way. Even follies replaced economically viable farmsteads where necessary, a far cry from Jefferson's attempt to enhance estate productivity within a Palladian framework.

The layout of Monticello might be aesthetically pleasing to the approaching visitor, but the outward distribution of porticoes merely reflected the internally efficient ordering of space for utilitarian purposes. The ergonomically acceptable machine or building was aesthetically superior to mere prettiness or fashion. The American landowner displayed his own taste and educated sensibilities as much as his British counterpart; for the American, however, these were dedicated to progress, a model that anyone going west could emulate for their own and, therefore, ultimately the country's benefit. Monticello in particular acted as a kind of filter through which only those elements of the Old World that were suitable for the New were permitted to pass.

Jefferson saw the American experience as an opportunity to return classical styles to a utilitarian state of grace. Monticello was to be no extravagance, but a working estate, a model for others, an experimental farm testing out ideas from which others would also benefit. Pope would have approved: "Tis Use alone that Sanctifies Expense ... Or makes his neighbours glad, if he increase'.[30] Monticello is an attempt to pare down the complexities of Palladian classicism, to reveal enduring values that would be of use within a republic, while developing architecture appropriate for a free people. Others might import prestigious classical styles to inflate and flatter their self-importance; for Jefferson, such grandiose schemes were a pretentious waste of time. While other southern planters increasingly sought grand estates to express their aristocratic pretensions, Jefferson sought a working show-piece for design improvements, much like a contemporary engineer might design and live in an energy-efficient home, or an architect in a new town. Space-saving devices, natural air-conditioning, efficient ice houses and appropriately located servants' quarters were developed and improved upon, all fitting together in a harmonious whole. Down the hill from Monticello, in Charlottesville, he designed a rationally laid-out campus for his pride and joy, the University of Virginia. Individual areas of specialisation were created, bound together through a continuous portico centred around the common library, all landscape elements fitting together within the rules of classical architecture for the practical benefits of scholars and their students. If kudos were to result for the architect, it should come not from the grandeur of the buildings, but from the worth of the intellectual community that such a scheme promoted, whether on a campus scale or across a continent.

A landscape suitable for a new republic

The new republic was no *tabula rasa*. There were already many contrasting landscapes scattered along its Atlantic coast, reflecting not just climatic variety, but also the varying societies of colonial times. But inland, especially in the territories acquired from Britain between the Appalachians and the Mississippi, there was great potential for starting afresh. Here the Founding Fathers could 'play God' and ensure a landscape fit for a republic. Here at last they could apply their enlightened principles on a grand scale. Indeed, beyond the Appalachians, the dominant feature of the western landscape today remains the regular survey authorised by the Founding Fathers, a survey still evident in property lines, county and state boundaries and, most noticeably, the roads. The Founding Fathers specifically sought to create an ordered extension to their new republic within their newly acquired western wilderness. To this end, survey must precede settlement to eliminate the chronic land disputes of the south's hollow frontier, where settlers grabbed what they thought to be the best without the benefit of adequate surveys, and where later arrivals moved on to distant spots, leaving miles of unclaimed and ill-defined land between clearings. A new system of colonisation would combine the ordered tradition of New England townships with the individualism of southern land-holding for the common good, while the principle of individual land ownership would ensure that New England-style communities would never dominate a wide swathe of the once public domain. Just as the USA sought to garner the best from the Old World, so it was right that the organisation of the western lands should combine the distilled benefits of eastern, more European experiences. Order in the landscape would encourage investment, family life, promoting a steady, ordered increase of territorial populations until statehood was reached. In a harsh and hostile world, there was an urgent need to create order out of revolutionary chaos. If western settlement could not be stopped, it must be promoted in such a fashion as to enhance the standing of the new republic. Jefferson's scheme for the Northwest Territory did indeed set the precedent for further westward settlement. Just as the political, administrative and judicial systems were to be ready

and available when further western lands, such as the Louisiana Purchase, were occupied by the USA, with territories becoming states on
a par with the original members of the union, so the grid system of prior
survey was also extended, wherever possible, throughout the expanding
union. The rectangular grid became *the* American landscape. Only in
very localised areas did traces survive of the French long-lot system,
mostly in the somewhat isolated bayous of southern, Cajun Louisiana,
or around St Charles County, Missouri. Elsewhere, pre-USA land-grant
traces have all but disappeared, much as did the territorial arrangements
of the native peoples. Over mountains and deserts, the surveyed grid
can still be seen, if only on the maps that, in some areas, still predate
settlement. The complex quilt of land holdings of the Virginia Tidewater
seems almost European in its complexity, compared to the triumph of
Euclidean geometry that is the landscape of the US interior.[31]

This newly emerging west came to reflect a wide range of late
eighteenth-century preoccupations. Selling off the federal lands, the
public domain, encouraged isolated farmsteads even as it inhibited
the emergence of compact and homogenous towns and villages, giving
today's Midwest and High Plains their own particular landscape. This
mathematical ordering of space was seen as potentially democratic: all
US citizens are capable of reason and, therefore, would want to live by
these laws of nature. A rational system would produce a minimum of
problems, while enabling ordinary people to exert control over the land.
Anyone could understand the basis of the survey system. It was not
arcane, nor was it the product of guarded mystical procedures understood only by a priesthood. It was open, honest and progressive – and,
therefore, quintessentially American.

Such landscapes, however, originated in theoretical drawings. They
treated the external world as a theoretical space subject to the rational
rules of geometry rather than to those of geomorphology or modern
chaos theory. Jefferson created a 'parchment landscape' in which the
complexities of the real word are manipulated to conform to the simpler
forms of geometry. It is widely recognised that these 'platted' (for the
map of what was to be was called a 'plat') landscapes ignored not just
existing native traces, but even the course of running water, vegetation
and soil types, despite the fact that these features were crucial to the
survival of settlers. More surprising were the scheme's 'flat earth' working assumptions. Complex geometrical adjustments of flat-plane
geometry were required to take into account the curvature of the earth,

which could not be ignored over such vast areas, by adjusting surveyed lines and lots. Adherence to Euclidean principles implied that lines of longitude were parallel, whereas, of course, over great distances they converge northwards. So, as with map projections that start with the earth's surface and manipulate its representation to fit the flat page, the Northwest Territory was surveyed as if it were flat and the results manipulated to fit a curved surface. The results are evident in those places where, for instance, four counties (or even, in places, four lots) should meet at a point, but are actually offset. This can produce very strange cross-country journeys on local roads, when what should be crossroads turn out to be significantly offset. More modern railways and motorways have returned to the principles of the old Indian pathways or the frontier droving roads, cutting across country ignoring the grid patterns completely.

Paradoxically, these precise financial and administrative procedures did not only encourage the commodification of land and an unprecedented passion for land speculation, but also provided ample opportunity for that most infamous of western institutions, the speculative settlement that might only exist on paper, as Dickens's character, Martin Chuzzlewit, found to his cost in aptly named Eden, more wilderness than garden. Maps had traditionally recorded what already existed. American maps presented what was to come. Confusing the two could be profitable or costly, depending on whether the newcomer was buying or selling.

Acting out the options presented by independence, Americans created a landscape in the west that still reflects those highly prized values of independence, mobility and rationality, forces that were to be as destructive as they were creative. The grid system enhanced more imperious, abstract and legalistic attitudes towards the environment which, once imposed further west on the desert margins, were to have major long-term ecological implications. The US constitution required the federal authorities to promote domestic tranquillity, wherever possible, in order to lay the foundations for a new golden age. Here at last, amid a surveyed and geometric heartland, Americans could ensure harmony between the good life and a willingly productive nature. Thus the Founding Fathers sought 'the smiling landscape of holy agriculture as an emblem of a morally and socially well-ordered estate'.[32]

But the National Land Survey in 1795 did not invent landscape rationality, nor was it the first such application within the New World. The Founding Fathers, however, had a novel context, the flat and supposedly empty Ohio country, where rationality could be applied without having to work around the kind of constraints that bedevil older and more treasured landscapes. But was the west specifically created to be a rational landscape? Or was it merely the outward visible sign of new economic rationalities and political expediencies, whose landscape implications were only later to become apparent? Only when motorists came to travel long distances and to need large-scale maps would the landscape's patterned logic become visible at all.

Notes

1. There is no study of Russian America that deals specifically with landscape impact and legacy, but these topics are dealt with in passing throughout James R. Gibson, *Imperial Russia in Frontier America: The Changing Geography of Supply of Russian America, 1784–1867* (Oxford UP: New York, 1976).

2. Cole Harris, 'French Landscapes in North America, in Michael Conzen (ed.), *The Making of the American Landscape* (Unwin Hyman: Boston, Mass., 1990), pp. 63–79, is an excellent introduction to this topic.

3. A useful discussion of the impact on the landscape of French life can be found in R. C. Harris and J. Warkeutin, *Canada Before Confederation: A Study in Historical Geography* (Oxford UP: New York, 1973). Carl A. Brasseaux, 'Four Hundred Years of Arcadian Life in North America', *Journal of Popular Culture* 23/1 (Summer 1989), pp. 3–21 is a good introduction to Cajun Louisiana, as is Marietta M. LeBreton, 'Arcadians', in Stephan Thernstrom *et al.* (eds), *Harvard Encyclopedia of American Ethnic Groups* (Harvard UP: Cambridge, Mass., 1980), pp. 1–3.

4. For a south-western regional view placed within a national context, see Stephen S. Birdsall and John W. Florin, *Regional Landscapes of the United States and Canada* (John Wiley: New York, 1992).

5. . David Hornbeck, 'Spanish Legacy in the Borderlands, in Conzen (ed.), *The Making of the American Landscape*, pp. 61–2.

6. Alvar W. Carlson, *The Spanish-American Homeland: Four Centuries in New Mexico's Rio Arriba* (The Johns Hopkins UP: Baltimore, 1990), deals with the impact and survival of those Spanish peoples caught up within the USA by the treaty of 1848.

7. There is a vast and growing literature on this transition. For an overview, see Stan Steiner, *The Mexican Americans* (Report No. 39, Minority Rights Group: London, 1979). For a comparative study, see D. W. Meinig, *The Southwest: Three Peoples in Geographical Change, 1600–1971* (Oxford UP: New York, 1971). A traditional approach can be seen in chapter 10 of J. H. Paterson, *North America* (Oxford UP: New York, 1989). For less of a textbook approach, see Joel Garreau, 'MexAmerica', in *The Nine Nations of North America* (Avon: New York, 1981).

8. For a useful overview see W. A. Speck, *British America, 1607–1776* (British Association for American Studies Pamphlet No. 15, 1985). For more detail, see J. Henretta and G. H. Noble, *Evolution & Revolution: American Society 1600–1820* (D. C. Heath: Lexington, 1989).

9. Douglas R. McManis, *Colonial New England: A Historical Geography* (Oxford UP: New York, 1975), deals with the landscape both implicitly and explicitly. For an impressionistic essay, see Garreau, *The Nine Nations* (though he maintains that New

England should now include the Canadian maritimes, ignoring the origins of the two areas on opposite sides of the American Revolution).

10. For an engaging, but none the less scholarly, essay, see Peirce F. Lewis, 'The Northeast and the Making of American Geographical Habits, in Conzen (ed.), *The Making of the American Landscape*, pp. 80–103. Almost anything by Lewis, on any topic, however idiosyncratically presented, is worth reading for students of North American landscapes.

11. There is a vast literature on the Mormon impact upon the Far West, though no one single volume focuses upon their landscapes quite like R. V. Francaviglia, *The Mormon Landscape: Existence, Creation, and Perception of a Unique Image of the American West* (AMS: New York, 1978). For a short overview of their desert landscape impact, see James L. Wescoat, Jr., 'Challenging the Desert, in Conzen (ed.), *The Making of the American Landscape*, pp. 186–203; and, for their linkage into the Utopian strand of US history, see James E. Vance, Jr., 'Democratic Utopia and the American Landscape', *ibid.*, pp. 204–20.

12. BBC Wales produced a 'jackdaw' style pack to accompany the schools series *Wales and the Americas*, which dealt with the settlements of both the 1680s, just west of Philadelphia, and the 1790s, in the Beulah-Ebensburg settlement of central Pennsylvania. See also Gwyn A. Williams, *Madoc: The Legend of the Welsh Discovery of America* (Oxford UP: Oxford, 1987), and *The Search for Beulahland* (Croom Helm: London, 1980), though landscape is dealt with only implictly.

13. R. J. Dickenson's 1966 classic, *Ulster Emigration to Colonial America 1718–1775*, plus a new introduction, has recently been reprinted (UIster Historical Foundation: Belfast, 1989). Landscape impact is more overtly dealt with in the work of E. Estyn Evans, 'The Scotch-Irish: Their Cultural Adaptation and Heritage in the American Old West', in E. R. R. Green (ed.), *Essays in Scotch-Irish History* (Ulster Historical Foundation: Belfast, 1969).

14. There is a large literature on 'The Best Poor Man's Country', as south-east Pennsylvania was often called, particularly on the various German-speaking agricultural communities. A useful introduction can be found in M. P. Conzen, 'Ethnicity on the Land', in Conzen (ed.), *The Making of the American Landscape*, pp. 221–48. For the Amish in particular, see the essay by John A. Hostetler in Thermstrom *et al.* (eds), *Harvard Encyclopedia of American Ethnic Groups*.

15. An interesting and illustrated introduction can be found in Randell Fegley, 'Plain Pennsylvanians who Keep their Faith', *Geographical Magazine*, 53 (December 1981) pp. 968–75. For a thriller set within the landscape of Lancaster County, watch Peter Weir's *Witness* (Paramount, 1985), famous for the restaging of a communal barn building to create a central element of the Amish cultural landscape.

16. Sam B. Hilliard outlines this point in 'Plantations Created the South', *Geographical Magazine*, 52 (1980), pp. 409–16.

17. Texan cultural variety and its impact upon the landscape is well documented. The most accessible entry into this material can be found in Bill C. Malone, *Country Music USA* (University of Texas Press: Austin, 1985; published in the UK by Equation, Wellingborough), where chapter 5 deals with the cultural and economic variety that has differentiated Texan music from that found elsewhere in the south or west. For a cultural geographer's more detailed treatise, see D. W. Meinig, *Imperial Texas* (University of Texas Press: Austin, 1969). If in doubt, read Malone for the most interesting geography of US cultural diversity yet produced.

18. Speck, *British America*, contains a useful summary of southern colonial life.

19. Robert D. Mitchell, *Commercialism and Frontier: Perspectives on the Early Shenandoah Valley* (University of Virginia Press: Charlottesville, 1977). For a summary of his main points, see his article, 'The Shenandoah Valley Frontier', *Annals of the Association of American Geographers* 62 (September 1972), pp. 461–86.

20. Tyler Blethen and Curtis Wood, Jr., *From Ulster to Carolina: The Migration of the Scotch-Irish to Southwestern North Carolina* (The Mountain Heritage Center, Western Carolina University: 1986).

21. Other states also cross the early east–west divide. New York has seen the frontier sweep over the Iroquois peoples, the fever of Erie Canal agricultural speculation, and the growth of Mormon expansionism. The original forest was cut down, while subsequent regrowth has been preserved for re-creation. Each era has left its mark. See John J. Thompson (ed.), *The Geography of New York State* (Syracuse UP: Syracuse, 1966), with an update in chapter 11 of J. H. Paterson, *North America* (Oxford UP: New York, 1989).

22. R. Cole Harris, 'The Simplification of Europe Overseas', *Annals of the Association of American Geographers* 67 (1977), pp. 469–83, offers a modern restatement of this version of Turner's frontier thesis.

23. David Lowenthal, 'The Pioneer Landscape: An American Dream', *Great Plains Quarterly* 2 (1982), pp. 5–19, follows up this notion.

24. J. Hector St John de Crèvecour, *Letters from an American Farmer*, published in London in 1782. Crèvecour was a naturalised French New Yorker who spent the War of Independence in exile in France. While in Philadelphia, he was a member of Franklin's Philosophical Society.

25. Thomas Jefferson, 'Query XIX, 1785', *Notes on the State of Virginia*, ed. W. Peden (University of North Carolina Press: Chapel Hill, 1955).

26. *Ibid.*

27. A point well made by John Stilgoe in his Common Landscapes in America (Yale UP: New Haven, 1982).

28. J. Adams, *The Artist and the Country House* (Sothebys: London, 1979). Hitler also succumbed to this vanity, appealing to peasants and *Junkers* alike as a wise landlord, master of all he surveys (portrait on display at the Imperial War Museum).

29. Denis Cosgrove, *Social Formation and Symbolic Landscape* (Croom Helm: London, 1984), p. 194.

30. *Ibid.*, lines 179–82 of Alexander Pope, 'Earl of Burlington'.

31. A useful summary is found in Hildegard B. Johnson's essay, 'Towards a National Landscape', in Conzen (ed.), *The Making of the American Landscape*, pp. 127–45. A more detailed exposition can be found in her *Order Upon the Land: The US Rectangular Land Survey and the Upper Mississippi* (Oxford UP: New York, 1976). Much the same ground is covered in Sam B. Hilliard, 'A Robust New Nation, 1783–1820', Robert D. Mitchell and Paul A. Groves (eds), *North America: The Changing Geography of a Changing Continent* (Hutchinson: London, 1987), pp. 149–71. The associated political and administrative arrangements for the interior are usefully laid out in Francis S. Philbrick, *The Rise of the West, 1754–1830* (Harper and Row: New York, 1965), with a concise and readable summary in Richard A. Bartlett, *The New Country: A Social History of the American Frontier, 1776–1890* (Oxford UP: New York, 1974). The cultural implications are explored in J. B. Jackson, 'The Order of a Landscape: Reason and Religion in Newtonian America', in D. W. Meinig (ed.), *Interpretations of Ordinary Landscapes* (Oxford UP: New York, 1979), pp. 153–63.

32. Cosgrove, *Social Formation and Symbolic Landscape*, p. 142.

CHAPTER 3

Cultural Landscapes of the West

Surveying the western lands, as the previous chapter noted, helped to tame the new territories. Even where there were no settlers, there were at least maps. The grid lines imply both that the land has been tied down under a great human web and that it can be cut up into manageable pieces. The land, in all its vastness, has become a resource base, one that seemed to be forever widening during the nineteenth century. This expansion of the country's development potential, at a time when there were not enough native peoples and settlers to develop it, made it necessary to continue to import people from overseas. Initially, these were mainly African slaves for the southern plantations spreading over the Mississippi into east Texas, but they came to include Irish and Chinese workers for the canals and railroads, Cornish for the hard-rock mines, Scandinavians and Germans for the farms on the prairies of the High Plains, and Mormon recruits for the valley of the Great Salt Lake. As railroad companies advertised their lands across Europe, people left for the New World in droves, seeking a new start far from persecution and the dislocations of European agriculture and industrialisation. What impact have these various groups had upon the contemporary landscape? Some would say, very little. For those who went out west, the federal government had already laid out the ground rules whereby land had to be surveyed prior to the acquisition of legal title. Territories from which states were to emerge were designated not by the settlers themselves, but by Washington politicians. What could the settlers do to sustain their cultural traditions? At the Chicago World's Fair in 1893 the historian Frederick Jackson Turner argued that such cultural baggage would be jettisoned along the frontier. Only those willing and able to act as Americans would survive, a theory with strong social-Darwinian elements. But it was often this despised cultural baggage that enabled people to withstand the rigours of the frontier and to find sufficient fortitude within themselves to carve out a place for themselves and their families within the growing American nation. The upper Midwest of today is as much a landscape of Germans and Scandinavians as of the

Founding Fathers' systems of surveying and government. Ways of life leave traces in the choice of crops, the decoration of churches, the names on war memorials, and even the array of signs on billboards and election notices. In the Dutch-settled areas of south-western Michigan, the absence of bars and picture houses is evidence of deeply held beliefs that distinguished otherwise similar ethnic groups. Evidence of this kind may be more subtle than the immediately apparent grid pattern of property lines, counties and states, but it is no less significant for all that.[1] In Texas, the presence of German and Czech settlers has contributed to a cultural landscape that is unlike that found anywhere else in the South. Racial attitudes reflect Texas's great heterogeneity, whether from its Mexican, and, hence, Roman Catholic origins, its settlement by central Europeans in the nineteenth century, or the influx of Americans from all over the country in the oil booms of the 1920s and the 1970s. The variety of church buildings, the mix of place-names, the diet and, especially, the music all contribute to make Texas quite distinct not just from the rest of the union, but also from the rest of the South.[2]

How did groups such as the Germans become so scattered over the country? Why did they not constitute a single mass of settlers in one state, which they could then have dominated, much as the Mormons did in Utah, or, earlier, the Puritans in New England? Each ethnic group arrived in dribs and drabs. Each new batch would be unable to settle alongside their fellow countrymen. Affordable land would only be available further inland, on a newer frontier. Only highly centralised and isolated groups such as the Mormons could ensure that late arrivals joined the main settlement. Less co-ordinated groups ended up scattered across the landscape, relics of a previous line of settlement. Land that had been settled by German speakers in the eighteenth century was full up when further German speakers arrived in the nineteenth century. The newer arrivals had to find land where they could, whether in Michigan or Texas. Precisely which part of the frontier they settled seems to have depended upon how they were recruited and, therefore, where they entered the USA. If they entered through a north-eastern port, the chances are that they went across the Erie Canal into the Ohio country and beyond. If they came in through Galveston, then Texas itself might well be their destination. Similar scattering can even be found tracing out the various stages of the colonial frontier. Welsh settlers found land initially west of Philadelphia, leaving names such as Bryn Mawr and Haverford on the landscape to this day. Later Welsh settlers had to move into central Pennsylvania to find affordable land, in what is now Cambria County, east of Pittsburgh. Neither community was sufficiently large to sustain the Welsh language into modern times. Only locally do culturally distinct landscapes provide traces of these vanished lives.

The cultural landscape of any particular place or region reflects more than just its economic role in the wider system, no matter how fundamental that role may be. Ethnic and racial groups *did* retain varying degrees of cultural autonomy. The Mormons represent an extreme attempt to retain both economic and cultural autonomy. In creating themselves, they also created a particular rural landscape of communal land and water holdings, planned and co-ordinated pioneer villages – all despite the hostility of other settlers, railroad cartels, and the federal authorities. When they finally accepted federal authority, the Mormons had been in isolated control for such a long time that it was their values which, nevertheless, came to dominate Utah. The very landscape that they had re-created both reflected and helped to sustain those values that distinguished them from other Americans. Later arrivals in the Mormon heartland had to accept the existing width of streets, the way in which water had already been distributed, the fact that bars were either totally excluded or restricted to certain, less than optimal, locations. [3] Groups with a sufficient critical mass in terms of numbers and political control can, even in multicultural America, ensure that later arrivals have to accept a cultural landscape that is not of their own devising. This can mean that, locally at least, the landscape reflects cultural values that either may not be shared nationwide or have been so degraded that it is only within the landscape that traces of their existence can be found. Place-names can reflect groups that no longer inhabit a particular area, such as native Americans; property lines may reflect the economic imperatives and transportation needs of long ago, when watercourses were the only routes, for instance, illustrating that the landscape often acts as a form of fossilised social relations within which people still act out their lives, but which they would never create if starting over again.

Most arrivals within the USA found that it was not only the political and economic framework that was already in place and, therefore, had to be accepted, in outline at least. Those who arrived first were able not just to set out the ground rules, but to establish complex procedures for their modification, thereby inhibiting changes that were not to their liking. The first settlers to make their mark upon the landscape, however, were not necessarily the first to arrive, nor even those who arrived in greatest numbers. To be what Zelinsky has called 'the first effective settlers',[4] involves a presence in sufficient numbers and with sufficient power to be listened to at that critical moment of codification of frontier society. For the USA at large, that was the late eighteenth century, most overtly with the codification of dominant political and implicitly cultural values in the creation of the US constitution in the 1780s. For the landscapes of the original thirteen colonies, the crucial period extended from the first settlement in the 1620s through to about the 1750s. For the lands across the Appalachians, the equivalent period was from the 1790s onwards, with the federal survey system and the arrival of the first settlers. Except very locally, the native peoples were ignored and their landscapes transformed. Later settlers who moved into the west had to accept those arrangements that were already in place, whether the location of international borders and state lines, the positioning of court-houses and schools or, more particularly, the privately owned landscapes of those who had arrived earlier.

The landscape of the west also demonstrates the ways in which a particular place represents a unique intersection of overlapping regional characteristics. Areas within the US grid survey were settled by different people, who would then respond differently to the national influences of markets and capital. The very similarity of western landscapes over such wide expanses often tends to highlight differences that might other-wise seem insignificant, such as the previous incorporation within discrete imperial realms leaving a different range of place-names in two initially similar landscapes, differing attitudes to water control distin-guishing otherwise very similar Mormon and Texas landscapes, and attitudes towards alcohol reflecting Roman Catholic and Protestant values and setting apart otherwise similar Texan landscapes (which still confuses outsiders, who cannot work out why one town is 'dry' and the other 'wet'). Each place is indeed a unique combination of overlapping and interacting processes, social, economic and ecological. It is in this study of place that we can integrate the unique with the general. If we do not recognise the way in which wider processes are expressed in the local landscape, then we are left with little more than a catalogue of landscape features for a series of unique and, therefore, unknowable places. Total outsiders frequently imposed sweeping and often inappro-priate images upon the west, however, riding roughshod over quite distinctive cultural characteristics. But just as the facts about the American frontier were never be allowed to get in the way of a good story about the Wild West, so local places were rarely allowed to interfere with the broad brush strokes of landscape as a uniquely American panorama.

The West and the image of America's wilderness

As the West became ever more vital to the US economy, so too it came to have a greater role within the imagination of an ever-widening array of Americans as politicians, administrators and settlers. By the 1840s, the USA had reached the Pacific. As explorers, government surveyors and, increasingly, painters (and later photographers) moved further westwards, the pool of information about western landscapes grew ever larger within society back east. Government policies influenced the areas to be scrutinised, pacified and settled. Expectations and commercial prospects frequently channelled the growing tide of frontier information towards specific eastern audiences, each ready to interpret and respond to these images in quite different ways. Painters and poets sought inspiration from news of wide plains and even higher mountains. In their search for a peculiarly American experience, here, surely, was the place, amidst the novel vastness of western promise. Here at last was a birthright appropriate for a new chosen people.

But the West was no single, stable image – certainly not just an image of limitless promise. In colonial days, whatever promise it held was more than countered by the immediate threat that it represented. Here was the home of Indian savages, of aggressive Roman Catholic Frenchmen, of bandits, escaped convicts and even dissenters, an echo of which comes through clearly into Hawthorne's nineteenth-century world. The wilderness might represent an escape from communal control for some people, but the forces of darkness waited for others, lurking to pounce upon the unwary.[5]

For entrepreneurs, though, the western lands held potential not as landscapes to be savoured, but as lands to be exploited. Initially, this involved setting up rendezvous points to encourage pelt collections from the native peoples. Later, the forests and the mineral deposits could be sent back east to feed the industrial revolution. Agriculture swept westwards as food and raw materials became more and more necessary. An economic empire came into being, gathering together the products of a wide variety of ecosystems and creating a landscape of contrasting human habitats and communities.

Was the West to be left as primeval wilderness or turned into a cultivated garden? The first option was hardly considered – at least until most of it was already gone. There was little dissent from the view that the biblical injunction to exercise 'dominion over the face of the earth' meant to cut, plough and dig, with scant regard for any environmental impact. Certainly, there was little or no interest in the aesthetic quality of the resulting landscapes. Yet the landscapes that did emerge, most fully developed in the forests and prairies of the Midwest, were a peculiarly US admixture of local pragmatism within the guidelines laid down by the federal authorities. This chequer-board landscape remains evident even where land has changed hands and lots were amalgamated.

The very scale of the American wilderness was often unnerving.[6] It is hardly surprising that the grid system was seen as essential to tame such otherwise boundless wastes. Awe filled those exposed to America's vast panoramas. Here was land on a scale unimaginable back in the Old World. Vastness alone emphasised the unique potential of the New World's premier republic. The purity of the wilderness, the extremes of hot and cold, all had a pristine quality that seemed appropriate for a new country that was claiming the high moral ground. Attitudes to this vastness, however, could be quite ambivalent: Walt Whitman could both praise the pristine, Eden-like forest in the 'Redwood Tree' (1874) while celebrating its destruction in the 'Broad Axe' (1858).[7] Walt Whitman celebrated the coming of the 'public road' and, in their classic prints such as 'Westward the Course of Empire', Currier and Ives welcomed the coming of the railways. All were indicative of what was deemed most progressive in the US experience – its restless energy, its expansiveness and the willingness of ordinary people to move on.[8] Thus was the special moral force deemed peculiar to the American republic expressed and confirmed in the novelty, if not uniqueness, of the physical environment. Uniqueness was, of course, asserted as self-evident. It was not the result of comparative landscape analysis, though there may have been implicit comparisons with folk memories from Britain. God, or history, had surely chosen this place for a specially favoured people. Here 'the last best hope for mankind'[9] would surely not fail.

As the USA moved westwards, ever greater sights were reported back east. Where the early republic had to make do with Trenton Falls, the Great Falls of the Potomac, and the Mammoth Cave in Kentucky, the newly acquired Far West had Yellowstone and the Grand Canyon.[10] Nature seemed less sublime out west, more magnificent. Either way, such sites of wild grandeur were both proof of America's favoured place amongst nations and places where New World citizens could feel the very forces of creation at first hand. Here the individual could finally escape the colonial cringe, that habit of forever looking over one's shoulder at the Old World, where history was more established, mountains higher and society more self-assured. The Far West was the definitive proof that the USA was a distinct experience, different both in kind and place from Europe. And all this could become evident by contemplating the wonders of nature (also known as 'the hand of God'). Each individual, as an American, could do this, enjoying and flaunting their vantage point from such high moral ground.

This view of the intrinsic 'Americanness' of the western landscapes has remained a feature of US preoccupation with the great outdoors. Recurrent interest in ecology (or what used to be called simply 'natural history') reflects a still-widespread belief in the restorative powers, whether for the individual or the nation, of the great outdoors, a view shared by such diverse people as the writer Thoreau and modern militia movements. Though interest can involve a retrospective appraisal of the west's role in the emergence of US attitudes towards the environment,[11] or the role of spatial images in the colonisation and settlement of North America,[12] the countryside takes on almost sacred qualities in an increasingly urbanised society. More is involved than simply contrasting the supposedly unspoiled natural world with the over-mechanised and brutalising world of violent and overcrowded cities.[13] 'Wilderness' has replaced nineteenth-century concerns for the American frontier, emphasising the purely American – and thus supposedly exceptional – qualities of such an environment:

> Americans sought something uniquely 'American', yet valuable enough to transform embarrassed provincials into proud and confident citizens. Difficulties appeared at once. The nation's short history, weak traditions, and minor literary and artistic achievement seemed negligible compared to those of Europe. But in at least one respect Americans sense that their country was difficult: wilderness had no counterpart in the Old World.[14]

Attitudes towards wilderness areas confirm the widely held belief that intrinsically American landscapes endorse America's favoured position. Most modern nations recognise that, though they may have wild and challenging areas, such as the Cairngorms in Britain, they have no truly pristine, untouched wilderness. The fascination with which Americans regard their last surviving tracts of wilderness has reached the status of a cult which seems culturally restricted to North Americans. As this cult seems to involve men (rather than women) striding off into the mountains to commune with Mother Earth, a cynic might detect a considerable Oedipal element, a desire to punish the dominating, exploitative corporate or governmental father figure.[15] Since modern population levels preclude ever having to live within the wilderness in all but exceptional circumstances, this cult may actually be a myth, indicative of the final death-knell of the western frontier.

The contemplation of landscape was one way in which individuals could penetrate beyond the immediate to more fundamental forces and processes, to become aware of the very essence of experience. Nature could spark a realisation that would transcend the immediate for the eternal, linking the individual with the universal. In a world of increasingly alienated labour, personal contemplation – whether of Walden Pond or the Grand Tetons – would surely release the aware individual's potential. And anyone could become so aware by virtue of being in America. Unfortunately, such a democratic right was rapidly becoming unavailable to the ever-growing mass of people working long hours in the factories back east. Even to those living in the countryside, the constant pressure of meeting the mortgage precluded contemplation of the wonders of nature. Nevertheless, the desire for knowledge (or at least understanding) through experience rather than through scientific, causal reasoning was to re-emerge from time to time as people sought an alternative to technically based industrial capitalism. By the end of the 1970s, when green pressure groups emerged within the USA, it often involved the evocation of pre-capitalist, analogical analysis rather than the seemingly suspect causal reasoning. The concern was no longer with landscape for the view. The scenic aspect was not as important as the environmental issues. The ability of an ecosystem to remain self-sustaining was more important than the purely aesthetic.

Landscape's one-dimensional scenic aspect became but part of a wider set of environmental and access issues. Renewal through recreation remained an important cause, though the low level of public access involved could leave environmental campaigns open to criticism from those who worried that 'Save the Bay' meant little more than save it for those lucky few who already enjoyed private access to it. This lament was nothing new. Once the United States had reached the Pacific in the middle of the last century, it seemed quite ready to turn in on itself and destroy those last vestiges of wild terrain that had escaped the encroaching frontier. Gradually, a wide and active conservation coalition emerged, including the hunting lobby of Theodore Roosevelt and his friends, which sought to create a sufficiently widespread level of concern amongst the educated American public to counter further threats to wilderness habitats. Their best-known legacy was the creation of the first national parks, such as Yellowstone (established in 1872) and Yosemite (1890). Campaigners such as John Muir argued that these remarkable areas of the public domain should be set aside in perpetuity for conservation and recreation; they should not be opened up to developers, as was the general rule, for here was America's own peculiar legacy, a landscape that none could match. Here future generations could experience some sense of what made America unique. Of course, designating an area as a national park did not preserve it from all change. Visitors required facilities; if not provided within the park, these would spring up at the entrances. Wilderness itself became a commodity. Once designated as areas essentially devoid of people (which, in the case of Skyline Drive and the Shenandoah Park, involved the expulsion of those who lived there), these wildernesses came to attract even more visitors; their impact has been so great that specifically recreational areas have had to be set up to draw attention away from the wildlife refuges and the real wilderness areas, open only to the hardy enthusiast or the accredited scientist. So, the meaning of wilderness changes with the times – from land to be civilised, to land to be protected and enjoyed, to land to be guarded against unwarranted intrusion – according to American society's changing concerns and priorities. By the 1970s, landscape, nature and the environment had almost fused into one all-purpose concept, somewhat misleadingly labelled 'the ecology' by the popular press. Even in the vastness that is the United States, those problems of access and conservation that we associate in Britain with places like the Lake District are all too familiar; except for Alaska, wilderness may well not survive the increasing popularity of once far-flung national parks in an age of affluence and mass tourism. Wilderness today is increasingly a managed resource, just like any other landscape, no matter how wild it may seem.

Notes

1. For a useful general introduction, see Robert P. Swierenga, 'The Dutch', in Stephan Thernstrom *et al.* (eds), *Harvard Encyclopedia of American Ethnic Groups* (Harvard UP: Cambridge, Mass., 1980), pp. 284–94. For their impact upon the cultural landscape, see E. M. Bjorklund, 'Ideology and Culture', *Annals of the Association for American Geographers* 54 (June 1964), pp. 227–41, and within a Michigan town, see John A. Jakle, 'The Changing Residential Structure of the Dutch Population in Kalamazoo, Michegan', *ibid.*, (September 1969), pp. 441–60.

2. D. W. Meinig, *Interpretations of Ordinary Landscapes* (Oxford UP: New York, 1979), is essential reading.

3. Mark P. Leone, 'The Evolution of Mormon Culture in Eastern Arizona', *Utah Historical Quarterly* 40 (1970), pp. 122–41, is an example of studies that recognise the way in which landscape reflects cultural choice for some, constraint for others.

4. Wilbur Zelinsky, *The Cultural Geography of the United States* (Prentice-Hall: Englewood Cliffs, NJ, 1973), contains a concise outline of his ideas on this theme.

5. Nathaniel Hawthorne, 'Young Goodman Brown', published originally in *Mosses from an Old Manse* (1846).

6. L. H. Graber, *Wilderness as Sacred Space* (Association of American Geographers Monograph Series, No. 8: Washington DC, 1976).

7. Walt Whitman, *Leaves of Grass* (1891–2 edition). Many of his poems express an excitement at frontier expansion that can seem, at best, naively romantic, but to read such enthusiasms is to touch a world that we may have lost forever. Note, too, that his images of the west are at least a contemporary voice from the America of the second half of the last century (unlike modern movies, which hark back to a mythical version of the same period).

8. This print's title is part of a prophetic line written by the eighteenth-century Irish cleric, Bishop Berkeley. Such sentiment seemed to evoke nostalgia even when it was first printed in the 1850s. Here is the neat frontier village, with its wooden school and church, the cheerfully industrious pioneers, the wagon road falling into disuse as the railroad speeds across the flatlands, making infinite the vastness of the west. And note how the Indians are cut off by being both on the wrong side of the tracks and hidden in the smoke. Yet most people who gave their pennies for this cheap chauvinistic print would never go west of Pittsburgh. For a collection of prints containing this classic, see *Currier and Ives: Chronicles of America*, ed. John L. Pratt (Promontory Press: New York, 1968).

9. 'The last best hope for mankind' is a rhetorical flourish much associated with President Reagan. The original line, in Lincoln's second annual message to Congress, 1 December 1862, was: 'We shall nobly save, or meanly lose, the last best hope of earth.'

10. J. A. Jackle, *Images of the Ohio Valley: An Historical Geography of Travel, 1740–1860* (Oxford UP: New York, 1977), followed by 'The American West as a Region', in his subsquent study, *The Tourist: Travel in Twentieth-Century North America* (University of Nebraska Press: Lincoln, 1985), pp. 225–44.

11. See, for example, R. Nash, *Wilderness and the American Mind* (Yale UP: New Haven, 1973). A useful summary of such ideas can be found in Alfred Runte, 'The West: Wealth, Wonderland and Wilderness', in J. Wreford Watson and T. O'Riordan

(eds), *The American Environment: Perceptions and Policies* (John Wiley: London, 1976), pp. 47–62.

12. J. E. Vance, 'California and the Search for the Ideal', *Annals of the Association of American Geographers* 62 (1972), pp. 185–210.

13. Leo Marx, *The Machine in the Garden: Technology and the Pastoral Ideal in America* (Oxford UP: New York, 1964).

14. Nash, *Wilderness and the American Mind*, p. 67.

15. Max Oelschlaeger, *The Idea of Wilderness: From Prehistory to the Age of Ecology* (Yale UP: New Haven, 1991).

CHAPTER 4

Landscape Painting

Americans like to see themselves as an essentially pragmatic, down-to-earth society geared to the promotion of unfettered individualism.[1] Certainly, the cult of individualism is real indeed. How, though, does this cult influence the US landscape? Most people would say that the enjoyment of landscapes is a matter of purely individual preference. However, the study of landscape painting, for instance, suggests that although images of landscapes seem initially to provide a particular, individualistic, and usually elevated perspective, such a privileged perspective remains socially created within specific historical contexts. The nineteenth-century fashion for landscape painting on a monumental scale suggests that the choice of subject and mode of representation were not the result of idiosyncratic, individualistic preferences. What was to be considered 'landscape', how it should be portrayed, and the effect it should produce were issues that were resolved socially. In the USA, the audience was a local élite that sought to confirm its growing preconception that exotic and fantastic scenery was not the prerogative of the Old World. Indeed, the size of the landscape paintings – and, subsequently, the scope of landscape photography – suggests that landscape artists shared society's growing fascination for the spectacular. As the US artistic community sought to establish its own independent credentials, it expressed its New World pedigree within wider, emerging notions of US exceptionalism, manifest destiny, and the cult of novelty. Landscape paintings were not just the neutral reporting of changing tastes, but agents actively engaged in teaching the wider public how to react to their surroundings, or at least to the westward lands.

Just as the Founding Fathers sought to establish both a new political system and a new landscape, so artists sought to build a cultural life appropriate for such a new republic. But how should Americans relate to their European forebears? Should literature, rhetoric and painting be reinvented, or should Americans build upon existing forms? Were techniques developed in Europe of any use in such a vast, new continent?

At independence, high cultural concerns – quite understandably – reflected European models, standards and expectations. The American literati still looked to Italy for its history, for classical and supposedly timeless styles. Looking at *View from Apple Hill*, ostensibly a painting of New York in the 1820s, the viewer could be forgiven for believing that the prospect was of the Italian Campagna and that the river was the Roman Tiber, so locked into European models was the artist Samuel Morse.

The European Romantic movement already looked to nature for signs of the divine presence. Where better than in the New World could artists encourage and indulge in an exultation of unsullied and primeval wilderness? Where better to draw inspiration from the mystical beauty of the wilderness and to experience, if only vicariously, a feeling of awe for the power of nature? Thus, although some views represented the vitality of life in America's growing towns, it was rural scenery that increasingly came to gain public popularity. Engraved volumes, such as *Picturesque Views of American Scenery* (1820) and *Hudson River Portfolio* (1826), helped to stimulate a growing interest in the American landscape. Thomas Doughty, for instance, travelled and painted the eastern states and was particularly inspired by visits to the Hudson River Valley. Though full of great detail, his paintings are far from literal renderings of what he saw; they are poetic renderings of scenes which, he thought, would express the ever-popular ideals of Romanticism – the passionate, the sublime, and the uplifting qualities of nature.

An English immigrant, Thomas Cole (1801–48), is generally recognised as the founder of the Hudson Valley school of landscape painters. His passion for detail implied that this was nature as it was, rather than in some idealised form. His concerns, though, were deeply Romantic. His study of the Connecticut River, *The Oxbow* (1836), executed in the studio though based upon field sketches, came increasingly to reflect the conflict between the popular taste for realistic rendition of the natural landscape and his own penchant for moralistic themes. On closer inspection, a seemingly realistic painting turns out to juxtapose pristine wilderness against a settled river valley, implying some kind of moral contrast. Throughout his paintings, there is a passion for the power of light to intensify the dramatic presentation of the landscape, a technique that he had learned from the European landscapes of Claude Lorraine and the etchings of Rembrandt. America appeared increasingly to resemble another Eden, verdant and full of potential, though whether

America could realise this promise remained an open question. After a trip to Europe, he returned intent upon creating a monumental series of large paintings, *The Course of Empire*, which would challenge, if only implicitly, the dominant progressive image of the American experience. All civilisations peak and then decay: why should the American experience avoid such a fate?

This was not a popular preoccupation. In fact, Cole's reputation may only survive because his followers developed a more patriotic genre from such inauspicious beginnings, working to exploit Cole's initial interest in the ways light could be used to explore American themes. Others began to range further afield, painting the Catskills, the Adirondacks and the White Mountains, though continuing to draw heavily upon the Hudson River Valley for their inspiration. After Cole's death (1848), Asher B. Durand became the central figure in what was increasingly seen as a growing, though diverse, school, linked only through a concern to study nature at first hand and to paint in the field rather than, as in Europe, in the studio. Durand's most famous work is probably *Kindred Spirits* (1849), which shows Thomas Cole and his friend the poet Willian Cullen Bryant contemplating the sublimity of nature. Two figures stand on a rock framed in the classical mode by trees and overhanging limbs, through which glows a luminous though distant sky, its light reflected in a tumbling stream below. Such landscapes are serene, full of atmospheric effect and precise in detail; great care is taken to suggest that the colours used were those of natural light, faithfully expressing the time of day and the season of the year. This luminist tradition came to be seen as part of a quintessentially American focus upon nature itself. Was not nature the outward manifestation of the divine presence, made visible by the artist? Here is a morality play of a different order. Direct observation was crucial not for slavish reproduction, but to focus upon its ideal qualities. The poet Emerson wrote: 'In landscapes, the painter should give the suggestion of a fairer creation than we know.'[2] As President of the National Academy of Design, Durand's preoccupations were to become America's new landscape conventions, exploiting European techniques for the presentation of varieties of light or the use of a human figure to provide a sense of scale in the presentation of American vistas.

But how did such landscape painters cope with the growing encroachment of an industrial world? Cole's sequence of views from the Catskill Mountains records the axeman and the railroad bringing an uncertain future with them, but was this civilisation or decay? Jasper Cropsey, noted for his autumnal Hudson Valley landscapes, increasingly portrayed industrial elements in a positive and optimistic manner, as in his *Starucca Viaduct* (1865). By and large, however, the representation of the urban industrial landscape had to await a new wave of social concern much later in the century.

Frederick Edwin Church (1826–1900), another Cole pupil, sought to capture the wild energy of the New World, seeking out remote places to capture the moment of observation. His paintings reveal an almost scientific concern for detail, allied to the dramatic portayal of natural light within storms, as in *Heart of the Andes* (1859). His first great success had been *Niagara* (1857), which startled viewers with its novel panoramic perspective from above rather than below the falls. Church believed that he should create canvases that were massive enough to suggest the vast powers of nature and that, with his scientific concern for detail, he could make the essential qualities of nature throughout the Americas accessible to all.

Explorers and travellers brought ever more spectacular natural wonders to the notice of their fellow Americans. Everywhere had sublime potential, but how much more so did the Rocky Mountains! If Trenton Falls, New Jersey, had once seemed dramatic, and Niagara Falls in western New York were incredible, how much more spectacular were the sights of the Far West, such as the Grand Canyon. Such sights were surely new wonders of the world, cathedrals of nature by whose side European artefacts and buildings seemed suitably puny. Where painters such as Cole and Durand and writers such as Thoreau and Emerson had once had to be content with exploring the transcendental potentials of the relatively tame eastern coasts and hills, the Far West evoked responses of quite a different order. Here was a land far superior to anything that decadent Europe could claim. If the English Lake District had problems competing with the Alps in the search for magnificent sublimity, how much more uplifting was the American west, with its mountains, deserts, and forests.

As expeditions scoured the western territories, artists as well as surveyors and naturalists went along to help relay the wonders of the New World. Albert Bierstadt's monumental canvases explored the gloom and glory of the Rockies, using light and colour and piling sweeping mountains and clouds into awe-inspiring panoramas which recall the European painters' need to evoke biblical blood and fire for equal impact. The distant wrath of God on Sinai could be experienced in the shifts of light and cloud amidst these western peaks. His *Storm in the Mountain* evokes the parting of the Red Sea, the land before the Flood, or even the Garden of Eden as the wrath of God emerges to drive out Adam and Eve. It was not only the Latter-day Saints who came to see the Far West as proof that here at last was a land uniquely fitted for a new and chosen people, a landscape ever more varied to which the USA had a uniquely justifiable claim.

Rather than appeal to the rational mind, Bierstadt used vast depths of scenery to capture mood and feeling. Nature's pristine grandeur surely reflects a divine order which can be experienced only intuitively. Amidst such grandeur, eastern rationality, such as Jefferson's grid system, seems inappropriate. As all Americans could respond intuitively to such marvels, appeals to experience, albeit vicariously, were more democratic, more American, than any theoretical view of landscape. Here indeed is a strong rival to the view that only a rational landscape is truly democratic. Instead, wild, uncontrolled, almost Gothic elements are deemed pre-eminently American. Here is the artistic wing of the frontier thesis: the Far West is the most American of places. Only here does experience expose those parts of the past that are worth retaining. Concern for the experience of the senses opens up the control of nature to one and all, regardless of previous social standing. The test, after all, is whether or not an individual is sufficiently prepared, innovative or flexible to become American. But were intuition and reason necessarily at odds? If each individual operated on the level of personal experience, those who survived and prospered would, in Darwinian terms, be the most fit – a rational outcome from an experiential rather than a theoretical approach to life. In fact, it was only by each individual acting without preconceived notions, almost without considering what they were doing, that the wider good could come about. Here is a role for landscape imagery that is entirely appropriate for the emerging world of capitalist relationships, paralleling, as it does, the belief in the efficacy of the unseen hand of the market which, alone and unaided, can make overall sense of the map of selfish, chaotic individual decisions. Landscape painters both reflected the concerns of their times and, sustaining a particular set of values, helped to promote and reinforce them, so that they came to be seen not as ideologically tainted, but just as the way things are, natural rather than contrived.

The popular view of landscape painting sees the artist as faithfully recording the forms of the external world for their own sake, resulting in 'realistic' landscapes. Modern landscapes, however, depend upon European notions of perspective, originally a technique geared to enhance the artist's patron. Perspective allowed such a patron to consider himself the 'master of all he surveys', as if everything has been provided for his personal appreciation. The power of such an image lies in its ability to present an individual, élite view as universally valid; the status of objective reality is claimed at the very moment that it becomes most partial. Such a way of viewing the world is, therefore, ideologically very powerful. A controlled perspective is presented as 'here it is, as and of itself, not as I would have it'. But the harmony presented is one of control, not anarchy. The harmony of such a landscape depends upon the perspective set up by the painter. In the American wilderness, this genre would operate within novel environmental conditions, but it would still seek to maintain a controlled perspective – as was to happen later with photography, a medium that seems at its most realistic when most controlled. The techniques of landscape painting allow – indeed, encourage – the viewer to pretend to be a fly on the wall, as if the landscape is being experienced not by an outsider, but by a participant, however passive. The illusion is complete: at the very moment that a subjective image is promoted, it seems to have a neutral, objective, non-interfering status.

In a nation increasingly engaged in treating the environment as an object suitable for exploitation, it is hardly surprising to find that landscape painting helped to prepare the US public for such an enterprise. Out in the wilderness, the very freezing of mood suggests universal and timeless values, whether in painting or in photographs such as *Moonlight, Hernandez, New Mexico* by Ansel Adams.[3] Americans' belief in their own pragmatism has tended to put great store by individual taste, spontaneity, imagination and direct emotional experience. These virtues were deemed universal and thus available to all, without regard for class or creed. In Europe, only those with appropriate sensitivities might be able to make the connection between the world out there and universal emotions; in the USA, however, such a liberating perspective would be available to all who experienced the western lands: 'Go West young Man!' was as much an invitation to experience the exhilarating, liberating 'feel' of the west as it was an injunction to frontier prosperity. Just as the panoramas on display back east had been deliberately created by the artist's choice of subject, perspective and juxtaposition of elements, so, too, had the experience out in the field. It was controlled by the authorities in their allocation of land, the location of government land offices, and the provision of protection. But people's experiences were also influenced by their expectations, and these were socially created within a specific historical context. Currier and Ives flooded the market with cheap chauvinistic prints which evoked images of progress, the taming of the wilderness, and the creation of an American landscape of farms and railroads in place of the marginalised, exotic native peoples.

Landscape, however, was not just viewed as a suitable subject for painting, on however gigantic a scale. The impact of the western lands upon society was not limited to the imagination of a few artists. Rather, it came to pervade the whole academic and learned community. The western lands were a series of ever-unfolding panoramas, an increasing, novel array of physical environments. How these new lands were to be surveyed and administered had long been settled by the Founding Fathers. Precisely how these harsh landscapes would come to be settled reflected not just the government's approved pattern of settlement or even the carrying capacities of particular ecosystems, but the ways in which the settlers themselves perceived the west before they even set out for their new lands. These images were created from a mix of image and expectation, including the artistic interpretations that affected so many easterners, whether settlers themselves, land speculators and developers, or government agencies. Images of landscape came not just to record the west, therefore, but to influence both the way in which people viewed it and the way in which they expected it to be changed.[4] Where once travellers had tried to ignore the mountains through which they passed, the scenic view is now the most sought-after in a train ride across the Rockies. Today's interest in scenery seems less than instinctive: contemporary travellers have learned to enjoy what once seemed uncivilised and, therefore, uninteresting.

What is the source of that pleasure, felt by so many people (residents and visitors alike), in the contemplation of the American landscape? There has been pride in the vastness of it all, whether plain, forest or mountain. There has been pleasure in relaxing within the diurnal rhythms and texture of the countryside. There has been excitement and wonder at the spectacular and unusual, such as the Grand Canyon, Yosemite's El Capitan, or Yellowstone's geysers. The sources of pleasure in the American landscape have indeed been many and varied, ranging from the satisfaction of pride to that of relaxation. But what stimulated these emotions of pride rather than aversion? Much of the sense of wonder experienced by the Founding Fathers resulted from a belief that beauty lay in the essential quality of underlying structures. For Jefferson, for instance, landscape was beautiful to the degree that it made manifest an underlying order. Equally, the human impact was beautiful wherever it, too, was based upon that fundamental order. Western settlement enhanced the beauty of the west to the degree that it brought the order of civilisation to the wilderness. Grid-based towns, rectangular farmsteads, regularly spaced facilities, all enhanced the Far West in the eyes of developers – a stance conveniently in accordance with the profitable potentials of the land.

As the landscape came increasingly to be seen as a human artefact, it became ever more open to aesthetic considerations. Initially, these might be confined to artistic representations of the landscape, which were then extended to landscape itself, especially where the Romantics' concern for the regenerative quality of natural landscapes was also evoked. How were the aesthetic qualities of landscape paintings to be perceived? Two stages need to be distinguished: the perception of the landscape by the artist; and the subsequent perception of the painting by the viewer (who probably has not seen the source landscape). Confusingly, the term 'landscape' refers to both stages for many people.[5] This problem of words plagues landscape analysis and has even led to the coining of new words, such as 'topophilia' (to describe a love of, or feel for, places).[6] Words of emotion that may be useful in religious painting are not necessarily useful in landscape analysis. Is a moonrise over a New Mexico village 'poignant'? If so, why? Others might see it as a trite juxtaposition of elements. Why is moonlight 'romantic'? To those who lived through the pattern bombing of cities during the 1940s a full moon probably suggests not tranquillity, but the vulnerability of sleeping people.[7]

Aesthetic qualities are supposed to reside intrinsically in certain geometrical arrangements of lines and areas. However, the establishment of these criteria is itself highly problematical. There has been a considerable attempt to apply to landscape the criteria developed for the appreciation of clothes, furniture, and buildings. But spectacular landscapes have been deemed too vast to be comprehended by such mundane parallels. The Romantics came to believe that mountainous landscapes evoked such strong emotions that the human mind is forced to recognise them as aspects of the universe beyond our grasp: the divine, the infinite and the sublime. Of course, the distinction between the classic appeal to reason (as a source of authority) and the Romantic appeal to the freedom of the imagination is nothing new, though the concern of landscape analysis for the 'picturesque' sometimes appears as an attempt to reach a middle path. It involves seeing in nature what had previously only been seen in paintings. The visual senses are educated to respond to the three-dimensional world as they had previously responded only to the two-dimensional representation of the world. But did American painters direct public appreciation and public taste towards the physical world, or did they merely focus attention upon representations that were divorced from the world? Or, again, did American painters merely display a susceptibility to the kind of visual environment in which the educated public was increasingly discovering aesthetic pleasure? For us the question remains: to what extent can we use art – in this case, landscape painting (and, later, landscape photography) – to explore not just the world of the painter, but the world in which the painter lived?

American landscape paintings came to be used as a yardstick against which landscapes themselves could be measured. The rules for the picturesque came to be as powerful in viewing contemporary landscapes as in viewing landscape paintings. If paintings were to be judged in terms of roughness of texture, irregularity, asymmetry, partial conceal-ment, the unexpected, and the impression of natural occurrence rather than of artificial connivance, then so be it with landscaped estates and, by extension, untamed, wilderness landscapes.

Irrespective of whether we believe our taste in landscape to be biol-ogically or culturally conditioned, there is a considerable tradition of explaining landscape painting in terms of imaginary lines of contact, pathways which link the visible elements into a cohesive whole. It soon becomes apparent when looking at any collection of nineteenth-century American landscapes, that clearly observed artistic conventions were in use. The feel of the landscapes, whether those of the Hudson Valley school or the larger Far West canvases of Bierstadt, is largely created by the mix of symbols of like, opposite, or complementarity. How these symbols are arranged seems to be governed by general rules which are clearly understood by both painter and audience; top and bottom seem to have their own specific associations, as do the flanks, which often contain symbols 'framing' the view. Such compositional conventions have a considerable pedigree, going back as far as fifteenth-century paintings, where the contrast between the centrally placed Madonna and

Child and the flanking vistas highlighted the strength of the central image of refuge. In more secular American paintings, caves, overhangs and forest glades came to suggest 'refuges', whereas the far horizon invariably suggested promise and prospect, the way forward to the frontier and the Pacific. Lines of sight draw the viewer towards a certain point, a geometric focus, suggesting a particular thematic focus, the point of the 'story' within the frame. The layout of the picture's elements, its compositional geometry, can move the narrative of the picture along. In the famous Currier and Ives lithograph *Across the Continent* (1868) the line of the railroad carries the eye to the western horizon, the goal of unlimited progress. The geometry and the narrative combine to reinforce the central point of view of the landscape: 'Westward the Course of Empire', the print's subsidiary title.

Western expansion was seen as the central objective, to which artists naturally responded. Lithographs of western images were patriotic icons which, like the flag, could be hung publicly to proclaim loyalty to the republic. The general public came to see as spectacularly American those images which painters had already accustomed them to consider thus. In a nation of newcomers – and in an expanding country, where even long-established residents were not familiar with newly acquired or distant locations – such a popularising of western images became very important. The vastness of the west had to be made intelligible, a particularly difficult matter given that even the Lewis and Clark expedition (sent across to the Pacific by Thomas Jefferson in 1804–6) found that their careful preparation in the geographies of Europe and the east coast left them unable to describe what they had found.[8] How much more was this to be the case for the rest of the eastern population!

Perhaps western landscapes were popular because they offered Victorians an escape from industrial society? Like the western movies that were later to promote particular images of the western frontier, landscape paintings provided an opportunity to place oneself, if only vicariously, at the mercy of the powers of nature. Here the city dweller could experience the taste of danger, brush up against safely contained primeval reality, much as in the white-water rides in today's theme parks. This search for excitement in a place of retreat may have started with the Romantics' attempts to escape from the modern world into wilderness. Most people today no longer seek permanent escape, but a period of uplifting relaxation, the oppourtunity to recharge the batteries.

It was not only painters who turned their attention westwards, however. The exploration of the Far West involved a growing attempt to catalogue and understand the vast amount of material collected by the geologists, surveyors, archaeologists and painters, to be joined later by photographers. Indeed, the Smithsonian Institute in Washington DC, the national museum of the USA, is based around specimens that were brought back to the east by just such western forays. The vastness, the scenic variety, the juxtaposing of spectacular and monotonous natural features, all fascinated an increasing number of western visitors, but also thrilled a growing public back east. The artistic conventions built up by the Hudson River school were available for those artists seeking to represent and interpret a west that most Americans would never experience. These paintings, geared as they were to specifically eastern concerns, are as much a window on eastern proclivities as upon western experiences.[9]

The technological innovations of the last century produced an outpouring of images, including a vast array of landscapes. Where once landscape paintings enjoyed a highly restricted audience (important social élites), the mass printing of etched copies, then lithographic copies, and finally photographic images in their own right, meant that landscape production became a great industry. True, most photographic images were initially portraits (for police files or as mementoes for relatives), but the easy use of the Kodak Brownie ('You push the button, we do the rest') meant that people soon could, and did, take snaps of the holiday sights (and sites). As the untutored masses snapped away, the professionals worked hard at perfecting new cameras that could take ever greater depths of field, wider angles, and, with increasingly sensitive film, be used under more and more varied conditions. Either way, the camera was a mechanical box which produced sharp, recognisable images which seemed uniquely unmediated – that is, they seemed real, neither subjective nor impressionistic. Taken to be a head-on slice of reality, this tradition came to dominate the production and acceptance of landscape photography in the USA. Questions as to who selected the particular slice of reality to be framed (and why) seemed inappropriate in the light of photography's supposedly self-evident ability to reproduce reality itself, to capture the very moment for ever, in images that were instantly recognisable and sharply defined. Photography seemed to substantiate the notion that landscapes were not interpretations of reality, but unmediated slices of reality. Sketches, maps, tales or trinkets, none could match the power of photographs, which increasingly appealed to a growing US public. Here was an 'abroad' within the confines of the union, not overseas as with Britain and its empire. What the grid survey could not tame the camera could contain, bringing all new territories (and their people) within the bounds of Jefferson's 'Empire for Freedom'.

While photographers of Yosemite [10] might approach the high sierras with aesthetic and commercial rationales, most early western photographers went along with scientific expeditions, providing an ill-defined auxiliary service to geologists, geographers and botanists. Earlier expeditions had had problems describing spectacularly novel topographic features, and painters might be too keen to infuse the western sights with a Romantic glow, but photographers could surely be relied upon to provide suitably scientific records of the region's natural history. US government surveys were supposedly objective, scientific reports, sent back to Washington DC, on these western lands now firmly within the union. Most expeditions were photographed, such as that of John Wesley Powell down the Colorado in 1871, even though, until 1877 (the advent of the dry-plate technique), processing had to be done almost immediately. Railroad track surveys might seem equally factual, but the spectacular landscapes produced by W. H. Jackson suggest an early interest in promotional images of use to his sponsors. The Denver and Rio Grande Railway Company were, after all, not entirely disinterested patrons when they provided a special train with a flat-bed car to serve as his camera platform.

The work of photographers in California was greeted with great excitement not just back east, but in Europe. The Paris International Exposition of 1867 awarded Thomas Houseman, Carleton Watkins, and Eadwaerd Muybridge a medal, and the *Illustrated London News* published a warmly approving review of these scenes of elemental nature: 'In none of these pictures do we see the last signs of man; not a log hut nor an axe-felled tree to indicate his presence: all seems wild, primitive nature, which gives the great charm to these excellent photographs.' Landscape photography was increasingly associated with the documentation and cataloguing of the native peoples. In the 1870s W. H. Jackson photographed and recorded the Pueblo people and the ruined cliff villages of the Four Corners of the south-west as well as the Pawnee villages of Nebraska territory, the latter images re-emerging much later in the ethnographically researched, though no less romantic, movie *Dances with Wolves* (1991). But what do such photographs actually document? Do they allow us to view the past in its own terms? If so, do we know what these terms were? Certainly, to modern viewers, frontier photography was used to take possession of the wilderness as much as surveying and map making.

A paradox emerges: survey leaders took along photographers precisely because the images that they produced were deemed a necessary antidote to the overly imaginative caricatures produced by artists. And yet Jackson's *Yellowstone's Scenic Wonders* was sent to all congressmen as part of the lobbying for its national park status precisely because this was a format that could make scientific research accessible to the public, simplifying reality to promote a suitable image of an American heritage that was worth protecting.

Most Americans travelled little around their country, despite greater rates of mobility than those found in Europe. The emerging images that Americans (and outsiders) held of their native land came increasingly from the landscapes presented in textbooks, posters, advertisements, films and, latterly, television, rather than from personal experience. Prints of western landscapes were initially, or seem to us at least, highly fanciful. Currier and Ives created popular images of western expansion, of railroads, and of the plantation south that came to encapsulate and promote very specific images of American life. Even the official US Geological Survey's scientific photographers were as likely to be engaged in work to thrill the folks back home as to inform them of western rock formations. In the long run, the impact of this plethora of western images was probably most apparent not so much in linking the general public with the scientific community, as in helping to romanticise and, thus, make accessible the complex finds of science, a necessary part of transforming western images into packaged consumer goods. In fact, new technical advances such as stereoscopes were a boon to the growing consumer industries, courtesy of the Sears and Roebuck catalogue. Looking at sets such as 'Alaska and the Gold Rush of 1898' and 'Niagara Falls' became popular parlour games and diversions in homes that were still without radio and television. Like the *National Geographic* magazine today such images were meant to instruct. The photograph 'Passing of the Indian' might appear nostalgic, though elsewhere the very same image turns up labelled 'The Triumph of Civilization', a far more forward-looking proposition. The image of the railroad trestle, the canyon and the native people remains the same, but the label provides very different narrative possibilities. The actual title to this popular stereograph was 'A Wonder to the Primitive Indian' – which sets a very particular slant to the way in which viewers are expected to receive and respond.[11] To complicate matters further, such titles were often chosen by the publisher rather than the photographer. And why was this image selected from the thousands available to be widely promoted? Did it capture both an aesthetic moment and a historically and ideologically specific one? Here indeed was an image which suited the promotion of a national image of technology and western expansion. The undisguised message was surely that those who could best exploit the wilderness would prosper.

Here, then, is the USA not only exploring the west, but reinventing itself in the very promotion of images appropriate for a continental power. The discovery and subsequent photographing of increasingly spectacular scenery in the Far West further emphasised US independence. Here was a unique series of landscapes, totally appropriate to America. No longer would travellers have to visit the Alps to see great peaks, high waterfalls, volcanoes and fields of ice. So popular were Carleton Watkins's (1861) images of Yosemite's El Capitan, for example, that anyone buying a postcard in today's national park is likely to recognise the picture's pedigree immediately. In 1884 the USA's first national park, Yellowstone, deliberately appointed an 'official photographer' to popularise an equivalent (and rival) set of images throughout the country. Even Ansel Adams's countless pictures of US national parks betray their links to these images of the 1880s. Yosemite's El Capitan is now a cultural icon almost as familiar as the Grand Canyon or Niagara Falls.

Whether movie-makers left New Jersey for California in search of better light or more amenable patent laws is debatable, but their sudden proximity to these increasingly familiar landscapes of the Far West gave a crucial boost to images that had already been widely promoted. It was the rocky outcrops of Monument Valley, rather than the muted hills and forests of New Jersey, that came to world attention through the films of John Ford and those who followed him, especially in the television westerns. An iconography has emerged of an American landscape – vast, heroic, yet tameable, inspiring an almost mystical, timeless awe. Spectacular scenery made more than just a convenient backdrop for the emerging movie industry: it established the movies as peculiarly American as the wonders of the Far West, unmatchable by any other country or industry.

Notes

1. See Wilbur Zelinsky, *The Cultural Geography of the United States* (Prentice-Hall: Englewood Cliffs, NJ, 1973), pp. 41–53, for a useful summary of American cultural motifs.

2. Quoted from 'Essay XII: Art', in *Emerson's Essays*, ed. Sherman Pane (Dent: London, 1906; reprinted 1971), p. 192. Emerson went on to suggest that topographical accuracy could be discarded in the interest of expressing what the scenery means for the painter: 'The details, the prose of nature, he should omit, and give us only the spirit and splendour [and] ... he must inscribe the character, and not the features ...' (p. 193).

3. A copy can be seen in *The Photographer and the American Language*, ed. John Szarkowski (The Museum of Modern Art: New York, 1963). Print shops across the world sell copies even today, disseminating a very specific image of the USA to people overseas. The original (1944) print sold for $71,000 in the early 1980s.

4. G. Malcolm Lewis has long explored this theme. For an accessible example, see his essay, 'First Impressions of the Great Plains and Prairies', in J. Wreford Watson and T. O'Riordan (eds), *The American Environment* (John Wiley: London, 1976), pp. 37–46.

5. For a useful introduction, see Kenneth Clark's *Landscape into Art* (Murray: London, 1949), which deals with the way in which landscape emerged from being the background to portraits, actions and events to become a proper subject in its own right.

6. Yi-Fu Tuan, *Topophilia* (Prentice-Hall: Englewood Cliffs, NJ, 1974).

7. Why should certain landscape conventions arise? Why should lakes be deemed to convey beauty, while mountains supposedly convey horror? Surely these are merely historically specific conventions? See Jay Appleton, *The Experience of Landscape* (John Wiley: London, 1975), p. 31.

8. Robert Lawson-Peebles, 'The Lewis and Clark Expedition, in *Landscape and Written Expression in Revolutionary America* (Cambridge University Press: Cambridge, 1988), pp. 196–230.

9. J. C. Taylor, *America as Art* (Harper: New York, 1976).

10. Weston J. Naef and James N. Wood, *Era of Exploration: The Rise of Landscape Photography in the West, 1860–85* (New York Graphic Society: Boston, 1975), contains a full description of early Yosemite photographers. See also Philip Stokes, 'Trails of Topographic Notions: Expeditionary Photographs in the American West', in Mick Gidley and Robert Lawson-Peebles (eds), *Views of the American Landscapes* (Cambridge UP: Cambridge, 1989).

11. Roland Barthes, in his *Images, Music and Text* (Fontana: London, 1977), has drawn our attention to the fact that a title can totally shift our response to the image.

CHAPTER 5

Interpreting Landscape Images

Landscape images help us to visualise the physical details of bygone days as never before, allowing the modern viewer to trace changes in the physical elements that created our surroundings without recourse to disruptive archaeological methods.[1] But, as with all images, US landscapes are shot through with cultural assumption. Only certain places and events were deemed worthy of recording, such as the Mexican and Civil Wars, the Klondike gold rush, or the novelty of the giant Pacific redwoods. Sometimes people fill the frame, squeezing out any residual landscape elements to produce a portrait. Sometimes the portraits are placed in context, as with the immigrant pioneers in front of their Nebraska sod homes, or teamsters in a Colorado street. Moving away from such intimacy, however, the photographer could contain a wide panorama, a whole prairie town, the Ohio waterfront, or even the Brooklyn Bridge. And the volume of material is overwhelming. Even those collections that have survived involve thousands of prints, usually unseen since they were taken. An accessible text such as the American Heritage's *American Album*[2] contains only two hundred of the five million prints within the US National Archives. What do all these images mean? As anyone who has tried to label or catalogue their own slides soon comes to realise, any one image can have multiple associations – is it an image of the clouds associated with cyclonic weather, or of Illinois farmland? Could it be a record of an architectural style? What are the focal points and messages encoded within these images or within the landscapes that they represent? Does it matter that some of them have titles, others do not? Do these images contain a syntax that we can decode and, if so, do the rules change over time? Do landscape photographs and landscape painting share a common syntax? Does the camera's framing of a portion of the physical world differ significantly from the more obviously created work of the painter? These are not inconsequential matters. Photographs are not peep-holes on reality; they are selected representations of reality. But whose reality? Western expeditions not only sought to establish US sovereignty, but often to refute or sustain a cataclysmic origin for the earth; their reports served particular agendas. Many sought to record a benchmark against which subsequent 'progress', whether cultural or economic, could be measured.

Expeditions across the Far West were not the last occasion on which the US authorities sought to record American progress. During the New Deal of the 1930s, the Farm Security Administration (FSA) used a photographic unit to chronicle its spread across the wilderness that was the Great Depression. Recording the underlying conditions would surely lead to the treatment of root causes, so the photographs were exhibited for public scrutiny and then published as book-length photographic essays. The best-known is probably James Agee and Walker Evans's *Let Us Now Praise Famous Men*, a 1941 study of two Alabama sharecropper families. In the pages of *Life* and *Look* magazines, such photographic images achieved popular currency, and people came to picture the Dust Bowl in terms of Arthur Rothstein's *Dust Storm, Cimarron County* (1936), readily available even two generations later on the cover of a Woody Guthrie CD. Photo-journalism, the movies and then television further promoted the creation of a nationally recognised set of images as to America the place, an integrated set of landscapes, whether positive (Hoover Dam) or negative (Hoovervilles).

The impact of such photographs does not remain stable. The reading of landscape images, like that of people, of movies, of newsreels, remains complex and ever-changing. Particular cultural values operated to create a specific image, just as other values help us to read it today. Do such images, once created, remain constant in their impact? The images remain with us, but the times that created them have gone. New values inform our reading of these images. Would the Ansel Adams photographs that so impressed Franklin D. Roosevelt that he finally agreed to national park status for the Sierra Nevada have produced a similar response from Ronald Reagan? Certainly, his Secretary of State, James Watt, seemed to see logging potential whenever he saw forests, and mineral rights in any mountains. Is it, then, the cultural context of the viewer that is crucial in any response? If so, this was equally true 125 years ago, when Timothy O'Sullivan worked for the US Geological Survey. Indeed, there is evidence to suggest that one of his aims was to produce photographic evidence to support catastrophic, rather than evolutionary, theory. His stimulus to action was deeply embedded within the scientific debates of his day, even while his images were more widely received in terms of the aesthetic sensibilities of the age, which they now illustrate. Even the so-called 'new topographers' of the 1970s, who tried to offer reality as it is rather than by way of their own preoccupations, merely illustrated current attitudes towards both suburbia and aesthetic theory.

With the transformation of the USA, albeit reluctantly, into an urban society, however, any consideration of landscapes, their formation and representation, must give serious consideration to the changing urban landscape, or 'cityscape', as it has been called in an attempt to focus attention upon the everyday surroundings of the vast majority of Americans.

Cityscapes

The modern US city is one of today's most familiar landscape images, thanks to the frequent use of the streets of New York City and of San Francisco in so many movies and so much television. The image is pretty stark: a huge, generally unplanned, teeming concrete hive of sprawling suburbs around a poisoned inner city, within which a regenerated core lives in a state of defensive alert. This is hardly a landscape appropriate for a new Zion or a city of brotherly love; rather, it resembles what the Founding Fathers feared would emerge from any attempt to harness cities to an American agenda.

The US entertainment industry, along with British-produced human-interest stories, news items, and documentaries, creates an increasingly urban view of US society, notwithstanding the recurrent power of western imagery. As the complexities of human anguish and triumph are usually presented merely for shock value, media images tend to produce, and then confirm, particular views of the US urban landscape. Studying the landscape of American cities, however, allows us to explore the interplay between images of the city, whether the glamour of *Dallas* and *LA Law* or the decay of *NYPD Blue* and *Seven*, within the built environment itself. The study of the urban fabric allows the landscape to be used much as an archaeologist would do, to work back from an aspect of material culture to the behaviour and values of the actors who created it. The hotel and convention-centre approach to urban renewal reflects rules that are central to the working of the US economy. The landscape thus created is the outward and visible sign of what are otherwise often invisible, but no less fundamental, processes of economic and, therefore, societal reproduction.[3] Landscape changes reflect US society's wider dynamism, identifying those forces which influence or even control the direction of change. The 'cityscape' today – using its widest definition, to include the whole of the built-up area – is the locus and product of an interaction between dominant governmental, corporate, and electoral forces and countervailing movements within US society. It is US society's main stage.[4]

What survives within this increasingly urbanised landscape reflects what is valued by those who exercise power, both now and in the past. Such power can be exercised explicitly – the decision to retain something such as the Old Post Office on Pennsylvania Avenue, or Union Station in Washington DC – or implicitly – the decision to invest elsewhere, which saved much of Savannah, Georgia, or Charleston, South Carolina, from nineteenth-century demolition. Most colonial 'townscapes' have been eroded to the point where few old buildings survive in the great industrial and commercial cities, though sometimes even here colonial street patterns remain, as in the financial district of lower Manhattan and in tourist ('heritage') central Boston. In Washington DC, 'colonial' Georgetown, despite some excellent examples of federal houses, is mostly late nineteenth-century residential development, albeit on an earlier pattern of streets, with only the Old Stone House, erected in 1764, being truly colonial. If Georgetown had not been incorporated within the growing federal capital, the town may well have declined, as did Port Tobacco in Maryland, now little more than an archaeological dig.

Despite a recurrent American ambivalence towards urban life, the great metropolitan centres of the north-east and the Midwest, plus the growing South and West, together contain over three-quarters of all US residents. Within the South, expansion has tended to exacerbate local differences; to trace the spread of its urban landscape is to explore an ever more varied southern experience. As people moved into the South, for instance, certain stops along the railroad became towns, while some of the South's scattered towns have emerged as cities. Crucially, an increasing proportion of its population, both black and white, now live within an urban environment, one antithetical to particular, though not all, expressions of the South's peculiar traditions. Texas, which first diverged from wider southern norms with its oil-based development in the 1930s, is now probably the most urban and, despite local loyalties, the most American of southern states today, though central Florida and North Carolina have caught up fast in the 1970s and 1980s.

The growth of supercities has been most evident between northern Virginia and New England, where competing yet complementary poles of economic activity have come to generate an urban landscape that is novel in both its extent and complexity – not a completely built-up area, but an area in which urban facilities are located in terms of the wider regional network of cities rather than the needs of any one particular city, and in which even green belts are geared to urban users, such as visitors, academics or researchers, rather than to agriculture. Similar 'megalopolitan' regions have been identified as emerging around the Great Lakes, from Cleveland to Chicago, and, even more spectacularly, along the Pacific coastline, where, by the 1970s, 80 per cent of the mostly urban population already lived in metropolitan areas of more than one million people. Perhaps this is the beginning of a peripheral landscape linking the Great Lakes, the Atlantic, the Gulf and the Pacific coasts, enclosing a declining, rural-based core of more traditional land-scapes.[5]

This contemporary situation had very fragile beginnings. In an essentially agrarian society, towns were small and, before the Revolution, over-dependent upon the imperial connection. Colonial New England, however, has been widely characterised as having a particularly important urban tradition, the landscape elements of which are the familiar church steeples, village greens and surrounding clapboard housing.[6] There was probably always a more dispersed landscape than this, later to be enhanced by a sprinkling of mills and factories along rivers and harbours. Further south, around Chesapeake Bay and along the Atlantic coast down to the Florida swamps, such entrepreneurially based urban expansion was generally thwarted by local planter élites. Charleston, South Carolina, was so dominated by the major slave owners that the needs of local traders and manufacturers were ignored in favour of neo-colonial residences for status-seeking landowners.[7] With business so constrained, such towns, though a vital link in Atlantic trade, failed to diversify and prosper as their northern competitors did. Their fabrics were not subject to the recurrent building booms of more dynamic towns, surviving almost intact as a landscape asset into the modern age of heritage preservation and tourism.

To Loyalist and Patriot alike, the towns of the late eighteenth century had become an alien and alienating landscape: the home of the mob, the unemployed and the unemployable. Towns should have no place in a truly New World, for they were constant reminders of Old World distress, power and social disharmony. Colonial ports like Boston and Annapolis were un-American places, the products of economic and political subservience – a view which conveniently overlooked urban revolutionary support. Some, myopically, expected them to wither away upon independence. Indeed, the US constitution ignores cities completely, as if trying to write them out of the script, while overlooking the power of those urban commercial and professional élites who were actively seeking to survive and prosper within the new opportunities presented by independence. In America's growing capitalist system, the expansion of trade and manufacturing meant that some towns grew apace – in terms of both the number and size of their buildings – Jeffersonian rhetoric not withstanding. Even so, a deeply felt antipathy towards these towns has remained a recurrent feature of US society and helps to explain why state capitals, with their gold-domed neo-classical architecture, were all too frequently located away from such unreliable centres as New York City, Baltimore and, later, Chicago (in Albany, Annapolis and Springfield respectively), as was the new national capital, Washington DC itself.

Anti-urban biases have also been promoted by American interpretations of the dynamics, impact and significance of western expansion. The popular image of the Wild West, created and sustained by popular culture, particularly pulp novels, the movies, and television, broadly follows Frederick Jackson Turner's thesis in 1893 that it was the frontier experience that distinguished the USA from its Old World forebears. According to this view, towns and cities arrived after the west had been tamed. Towns, however, were spearheads of western settlement, an intrinsic part of the frontier, whether garrisons, rendezvous, mining centres or railheads.[8] Admittedly, many of these towns were ephemeral: the forts were dismantled, the beaver were exterminated, or the lode ran out. Their transitory nature usually inhibited the development of sufficiently strong local loyalties to ensure survival in changed circumstances, a motif that is explored in movies such as George Steven's *Shane* (1953), Robert Altman's *MacCabe and Mrs Miller* (1971), Clint Eastwood's *High Plains Drifter* (1973) and Michael Cimino's *Heaven's Gate* (1980). If living in towns should become unavoidable, then everything possible should be done to make the surroundings seem as rural, if not rustic, as possible – a sentiment to be exploited by suburban developers.[9]

Within the growing industrial centres, a unique urban landscape emerged at an unprecedented rate. Commercial needs for appropriate premises, manufacturers' needs for greenfield sites adjacent to transport routes, and workers' needs for access to cheap housing and the unskilled job market, all combined to produce a new social and economic landscape. The urban élite resolved the problem of how to take part in the growing wealth of cities while remaining quarantined from threats to public order by retreating either to new suburban districts or to tight inner-city enclaves (the forerunners of today's Beacon Hill, Boston and Georgetown in Washington DC), leaving the labouring classes crowded together near their often noxious sources of work, such as the slaughterhouse, the glue factory or the blast furnace. Within the eastern USA, over 80 million people now live in the great conurbations of the Boston–Washington DC–Chicago triangle; a cursory view is enough to suggest that these cities reveal their late nineteenth-century expansion rather than their colonial or early national foundations. How did this expansion come to eliminate most of the evidence of earlier settlement? Before the great industrial boom of the last century, places such as Williamsburg, the capital of Virginia, reflected the expansion of imperial trade, linking British subjects with the imperial authorities and Atlantic traders with the opening interior. To the west, centres like El Paso and Albuquerque played similar roles within the Spanish lands. To survive the trading dislocations of independence, towns had to adjust or decline. In the search for interior routes of trade, whether by packhorse (the famous Yankee peddler), by canal (the Erie from the 1820s), or by railroad (such as the Baltimore and Ohio from the 1830s) some commercial cities such as Boston, New York City and Baltimore prospered at the expense of once vibrant colonial ports such as Annapolis, Georgetown, and Port Tobacco in Maryland, Alexandria, Jamestown or Yorktown in Virginia.

Northern cities became links in a new system of world trade, and New York City came to control both exports and the market penetration and exploitation of an ever-widening western resource base. To ensure continuing profitability, investors needed to seek out reinvestment opportunities, hence the popularity of schemes promoting new transportation technologies, new forms of processing raw materials, and manufacturing. This growth in trade and industry taxed the ability of existing towns – their numbers, their locations and their internal layouts – to cope with such novel pressures. From a population of 30,000 in 1830, Chicago grew to over 300,000 in 1850, and by the World's Fair of 1893 was able to boast over one million inhabitants. What had taken generations to achieve in London took place here within a single lifetime. In the chaos of such transformations, little was deemed sacrosanct. Chicago has little from its early beginnings. Even its Dearborn railroad station, a faint echo of Fort Dearborn, is no more. The 'Great Chicago Fire' of 1871 completed in three days only what would have happened in a decade or so of demolition and building. Here were no sacred places. George Washington did not sleep here! Most immigrants left decaying neighbourhoods as soon as education and a good job would permit. Downtown was a place to work, not to sanctify. New technologies necessitated new sites. Factories were built and re-sited. Slums came and went. The slaughterhouses that characterised south Chicago for so long are now but a memory.[10] Back east, towns grew up on the coalfields, great Rhondda-like scars on the Appalachian landscape. Gaining a wider hinterland was crucial, but an appropriate urban fabric was also essential to the promotion and maintenance of profitability.[11] However important Philadelphia's river frontage, Boston's peninsula, or Manhattan's island in promoting or containing expansion in idiosyncratic ways, a city's growth depended not just upon considerations of site, but upon how flexible that city could become. Adjusting the urban landscape is no easy task, for it is the product of many individuals and institutions, not always working in concert. Furthermore, a townscape created at a particular stage in a city's development is not necessarily adequate or appropriate for later use. The colonial and early national townscapes were simply not up to fulfilling the needs of nineteenth-century growth. The blighting of specific neighbourhoods by adjacent noxious facilities such as slaughterhouses and blast furnaces or by the creeping dereliction around expanding docks, warehouses and railroad yards threatened ever larger areas of housing, encouraging more of the the middle classes to leave for new properties. A cycle of construction and destruction engulfed the housing around the emerging central business district. Businesses such as accountancy and publishing congregated around government and legal offices, as did banks, insurance and investment companies.[12] Each new building brought jobs into the city, encouraging day labourers to live as close as possible to construction sites, the wharves and the new factories. The creation of one landscape involved the gradual destruction of its immediate forebear. The face-to-face relationships of the pedestrian city were inappropriate – if not dysfunctional – for the emerging needs of the new urban élites, who moved away. In their need for access to varied sources of employment and cheap housing, immigrants were restricted to decaying or jerry-built housing. They seemed to be crowding out any remaining white, Anglo-Saxon Protestants, creating ethnic neighbourhoods that seemed, to the casual observer, little more than slums, bars and synagogues, an Old World Babel dangerously close to vibrant business districts. Many central cities still demonstrate their nineteenth-century origins and heritage not just in their ethnic neighbourhoods, such as Italian south Philadelphia or Irish south Boston, but in their grandiose city halls (Milwaukee), their universities (Chicago), and their corporate headquarters (Baltimore's Seltzer Tower, the forerunner of today's Sears Tower in Chicago).

Beyond the central city, entrepreneurs left their mark upon both a wide and expanding zone of industrial activity, served by vast areas of cramped housing, and a more distant, but equally expansive, suburbia of single-family housing, each on its own lot, linked by extensive networks of streetcars (trams) and suburban railroads – the basic nineteenth-century landscape bequeathed to the modern city. Though individual buildings have been pulled down, the basic outlines remain intact, especially in the seemingly anachronistic proximity of great public and private wealth to utter squalor, the remnants of once vibrant immigrant neighbourhoods.

The modern suburban landscape

The construction of a toll-free motorway system throughout the USA after 1945 was to revolutionise the post-war American landscape, replacing the national railroad system with motorways, contributing to the modern suburbanisation of society far beyond anything envisaged in the days of the streetcar. Though these freeways were designed initially to link states, their most visible impact was around individual cities, for these new highways were soon being used by city workers to commute into the city from purpose-built dormitory suburbs. Once the US authorities had provided great arterial routes out of the old cities, developers and local municipalities could provide the link between the exit ramps and the new houses. The key was a steady supply of affordable housing in the newly opened-up areas.

With the shift to a Cold War consumer economy, the construction of new housing was promoted by encouraging mortgage ('saving and loan') institutions to take out government insurance, leading to cheaper mortgages and the sale of more homes. Mortgages would only be insured for new greenfield sites, however. The focus of urban investment, both individual and corporate, was turned away from the decaying, inner cities to the suburban periphery. Conversely, the existing inner-city housing areas became stuck in a downward spiral of disinvestment and decay. When the rules were changed twenty years later, it was already too late. The suburbs were now self-governing, beyond the jurisdiction of the inner cities, and able to deter would-be arrivals by zoning regulations which excluded the types of accommodation that these newcomers sought, like flats and small, single-family homes. The suburban landscape was a defendable space, more secure than any moated castle could ever be.

City growth has never been just more of the same. It is a complex, cumulative interaction between the re-sorting of existing facilities and the creation of new enterprises; the result is a constant jostling for suitably advantageous sites and locations. Though the first shopping mall was opened as early as 1923 (outside Kansas City) and, within a decade, Sears and Roebuck were opening branches outside city centres, the central city nevertheless retained its dominance in business and retail activity until the 1950s. When growth was restored to the domestic market after 1945, this same complex interplay was resumed on a larger canvas, using newly developed technological and managerial skills to enhance profitability by activating a long pent-up demand for new premises, housing and consumer goods. The collapse of the urban construction industry in the 1930s had been not only a vivid manifestation of overall economic collapse, but an essential part of it; its legacy was a run-down urban landscape deeply in need of massive investment, both public and private.

Even before the First World War, factories had followed the railway lines beyond the increasingly congested central city to cheaper sites beyond the fledgling suburbs. Here satellite and company towns had been served either by reverse commuting or by the provision of purpose-built accommodation where workers could be protected from the evils of the city. During the 1920s, railroad-dependent industries had looked for suitable sites on the periphery of many cities. Such factors as the advent of the truck, the extension of power grids, and the increasing need for large blocks of cheap land for horizontal mass-production techniques already pointed to the potential of peripheral greenfield sites.

Though post-1945 suburbs might initially have been dormitory developments, they did not remain so for very long. The massive shift in the location of skills, higher disposable incomes, and votes brought about corresponding business and political readjustments. Citizens required roads, sewage connections, water supplies and schools, and these all cost money, making it necessary to broaden the suburban tax base. Shopping centres, business parks, colleges and high-tech industries were attracted to suburban greenfield sites which could offer access to the interstate freeway network. As services expanded, people moved to the suburbs in search of jobs, until the suburbs were no longer dormitory commuting areas. Traffic congestion, further highway construction, even industrial pollution, all have emerged throughout suburbia, stimulating a movement to newer, more expensive and, therefore, more select suburbs further out, starting up the process all over again.[13]

These forces, which became so apparent in the 1960s and the 1970s, have not only reinforced and accelerated the continuing shift of economic activity – often beyond the outer ringroads (beltways) – but have also involved the abandonment of the central areas by all but the very rich and the very poor. The metropolitan electorate is increasingly a suburban one. By 1970, more than half of the American metropolitan population already lived outside the central cities, rising towards two-thirds by 1990. This shift of political and economic power alone would have placed the inner cities in an increasingly untenable position. But the 1950s had seen an era of massive downtown destruction, euphemistically called 'urban development'. The Housing Act of 1949 funded slum clearance by subsidising sites for developers. Those unable to move to the suburbs found a contracting rental market over which they had no influence, with redevelopment projects under the control of local business interests – construction firms and estate agents who positively disliked municipal housing and had not yet discovered the profitable potentials of renovation. A 'federal bulldozer' was needlessly and fatally tearing out the heart of healthy, albeit unfashionable, neighbourhoods.[14] In the early 1970s, the Vietnam War siphoned off the tax dollars that could have brought about comprehensive inner-city renewal, and the advent of the Nixon–Reagan era ushered in a 'benign neglect' that the Carter interlude was unable to thwart, despite the Democrats' overt concern for urban problems.

Inner-city redevelopment

For the past thirty years, the suburban shopping precinct (mall) has been the centre of commercial and retail activity for most people. By the 1980s, over 20,000 malls had already been built throughout the USA, of which over 1,000 were of the newer, climate-controlled generation, with 200 stores per site, and usually providing banks, post offices, libraries and cinemas – a complete alternative to downtown, which, in its turn, has attempted to compete with smaller, often more specialised, malls. Some cities have pedestrianised existing shopping areas on the European model, such as Chicago's State Street, or they have developed brand-new complexes on cleared sites, such as The Market in midtown Manhattan. Philadelphia's Gallery, costing $125 million, involved a multi-level mall next to City Hall. Further commercial successes have followed in old warehouses by the Baltimore and Ohio Canal in George-town, an up-market district of Washington DC, providing a very European urban setting in the heart of the USA.

The rationale for such projects has been to provide a catalyst for further inner-city revitalisation. The original development poles were such public centres as Boston's Government Center, Hartford's Constitution Plaza, and the Charles Center immediately adjacent to Baltimore's inner harbour. These publicly underwritten projects were deemed essential as symbolising civic commitment to inner-city survival, setting an appropriate tone for further development. Mall promoters were less anxious about their investment if it was part of an already vibrant development. Conference and convention centres such as Chicago's McCormack Center were developed in conjunction with new downtown hotels, often part of the Hilton, Hyatt, and Marriott chains. City governments pushed hard for these investments as the cornerstone of inner-city revitalisation, though these prestigious commercial and retail developments have tended to bring disproportionate benefits to a small and affluent segment of society. As the destruction of Washington DC's Foggy Bottom slums led to the construction of the Watergate complex of exclusive flats and offices – benefiting the cosmopolitan élite rather than providing affordable homes for the displaced black residents – so the inner-city speciality malls, like those within Detroit's Renaiss-ance Center,[15] may appeal to city élites – young childless professionals, tourists and convention visitors – rather than provide anything beyond

dead-end, unskilled jobs for inner-city residents. Even some revitalisation projects are not as secure as might be hoped. Detroit's Renaissance
Center seemed to involve the relocation of existing businesses within
the defendable space that it provided, rather than the generation of any
significant new investment. Even Baltimore's prestigious Inner Harbor
has still to generate a return on its massive public investment, remaining
a huge public subsidy for private enterprise.[16] This is particularly ironic,
as such projects actually turn public space – roads, pavements and
markets, with almost unlimited public access at all hours of the day and
night – into private domains to which the public have no right of access
and from which they can be excluded with scant regard for normal rights
of passage and free association.[17] So-called 'streets' within such facilities
can be shut by the operator without recourse to normal procedures and
without concern for the effect of this closure of access routes on adjacent communities. The facility just shuts, like the private shop that it
really is.

As suburbs came increasingly to resemble the cities, and as many
upwardly mobile people became apprehensive about their isolation in
far-flung suburbs, downtown was looked at once again as a potential
housing area. Regeneration here had started to provide both professional
jobs and up-market accommodation, if only within those areas under-
going 'urban homesteading', whereby young professionals are
encouraged to buy dilapidated properties at knock-down prices and then
to do them up to building-code standards. Areas like Federal Hill in
Baltimore and Capitol Hill in Washington DC have, in effect, been
taken over from the previously poor, black and tenant occupiers. Once
'red-lined' neighbourhoods, where loans were simply not available for
black residents, they are now miraculously revalued as ripe for investment. Gentrification has been very successful in transforming retail
business, raising the local tax base, and, particularly, in renovating the
urban fabric, but at great cost for those displaced into the declining
rental market. Caught between encroaching gentrification and suburbs
closed to all but the black middle class, larger numbers of black people
have been forced into overcrowded, decaying and dead-end neighbourhoods, such as Anacostia in Washington DC, and Roxbury in Boston.
Away from certain pilot projects, New York City's South Bronx
resembles 1945 Berlin; parts of inner Cleveland resemble those imaginary
post-Holocaust cities where grass grows in the streets. Even in many
Sunbelt cities, far too many inner-city neighbourhoods resemble

Carpenter's *Assault on Precinct 13* rather than Spielberg's suburban port of call in *ET*.

New York City: the growth of an urban icon

The most familiar image of any US city must surely be the New York City skyline. How was this unique assemblage of buildings brought about, and how did it become so familiar to so many people? Dominating both the transatlantic trade routes and access into the interior, business flourished here as in no other city. Building booms dramatically changed the face of the waterfront and broke the traditional links between places of business and places of residence. The island of Manhattan offered miles of waterfront, enabling the building of new warehouses and manufacturing facilities away from the traditional location of business. Commerce, in contrast to transhipment and manufacturing, could remain around the old town south of Wall Street. By the late 1870s, however, lower Manhattan's skyline still had more in common with Hanseatic Europe than with today's famous profile, produced by a transformation which was symbolised by the opening of the Brooklyn Bridge in the 1880s, giving the growing middle classes easier access to substantial urban communities on Long Island. In similar fashion, railroad links across the Harlem River to the Bronx opened up new territories for the development of purpose-built family homes, from which the lone, male breadwinner commuted daily into the city. Initially, suburban expansion had been very select. But real-estate developers were soon eager to encourage and facilitate the creation of a mass demand for their product. To this end, the rural, nostalgic, anti-urban biases with which potential buyers were familiar could be manipulated to enhance the positive features of the new suburbs, even when developers came to meet mass demand with tenements, as in the South Bronx. Movement to the suburbs was proof of individual success and, paradoxically, a reaffirmation of traditional values. The extension of city-based services and public utilities to these new suburbs meant that the only limit upon expansion became the walking distance to the nearest station or streetcar stop.[18] This resulted in nodes, and then fingers, of development along these arterial routes, between which lay market gardening and open country-side, at least until the arrival of the motor car brought in-filling of these open green spaces.

Such developments were only possible within the wider industrialisation of US society, providing entrepreneurs with the appropriate
technological innovations, such as cheap railways, switching gears and
engines of sufficient power. And it was precisely this industrial transformation that enabled New York City to emerge with a unique skyline,
as technological innovation was placed at the service of corporate
rivalry.[19] Frame construction techniques enabled the new, purpose-built
office blocks downtown to rise far beyond their previous structural limits
of four or five floors. Carrying the load on steel skeletons meant that
walls became mere cladding, keeping out the elements rather than
bearing the load. The development of water pumps, elevators and fire-
escapes enabled the full potential of ever taller buildings to be realised.
Corporate prestige benefited from association with the newest, the tallest,
the most innovative building, and competition for the most prestigious
central location meant that rents rose, driving out those businesses and
residences which could be located elsewhere. The central business district was consolidated by the proximity of public buildings such as
museums and galleries and concert halls like Madison Square Gardens
and the Metropolitan Opera. Signs of rival authority survived with the
landscape, such as Tammany Hall and St Patrick's Cathedral, both
increasingly engulfed, though within the skyscrapers that came to char-
acterise New York City by the 1930s.

How did New York City's urban landscape come to be familiar to
so many? As photographers tried to come to terms with the spectacular
novelty of the west, something remarkably similar emerged in the growing industrial cities in the east. Trying to make sense of the increasingly
sprawling, polyglot, and impressive cities, photographers created a
wealth of images that ranged over the changing landscape: the railroad
network, the docks, the new bridges, and the exotic ethnic neighbourhoods. Joshua H. Beal's composite panorama of southern Manhattan,
taken from the newly constructed Brooklyn Bridge's eastern pier in
1876, helped to move the city photograph from a rather staid, full-frontal
record of the public face of particular buildings to a wider swathe of
cityscape.[20] Our familiarity with the images of a city that most of us
have never visited suggests that, nevertheless, we are linked into a
network that presents New York as an image that is vital to our experience as modern people. It can hardly be a coincidence that the one city
to become so well known was, until comparatively recently, the major
link between the Americas and the outside world. The spectacular site

of the islands at the mouth of the Hudson River enhances equally spectacular landscape elements, particularly the Statue of Liberty,[21] the skyscrapers,[22] and the bridges,[23] all of which are part of the experience of many generations of immigrants and visitors alike. And, like such rural icons as Niagara Falls, the images of New York City's skyline have been produced and reproduced again and again, individually and collectively, from cheap prints of the Brooklyn Bridge to Woody Allen's movie *Manhattan*, by way of television's *Kojak*, *Cagney and Lacey*, and even the deliberately eye-catching and scene-setting opening images of *Friends*, to every documentary or news item from the city. No other city can present such a recognisable profile, with the possible exception of San Francisco's Golden Gate Bridge, cable cars, and Bank America building. Despite years of *Dallas* and *LA Law*, few would recognise the skyline of Dallas or Los Angeles as the world recognises New York. Most other US skylines are so undistinguished that television producers can use Canadian backdrops, as in *The X Files*, and pass them off as US locations (so saving on more expensive US location costs).

Does the urban landscape overtly include its people? The question is more vital, perhaps, in the more populated towns and cities. Are subway riders part of the landscape, or will their departure reveal the landscape? Walker Evans's studies of Detroit street scenes emphasise the place of work, its necessary context, exploring the relationship between people and place. Studies of rising skyscraper canyons often deliberately exclude puny individuals, emphasising city or corporate power in the face of personal insignificance.[24] Framing an image not only freezes a particular moment, but focuses upon a particular vantage point. Meaning can then be controlled further by cropping, for relationships between component parts of the image have a geometry and, therefore, a force quite independent of any set of relationships that they might or might not have had in the full, orginal image and, more especially, in reality. Change the frame (by re-cropping), and the internal geometries are manipulated, independent of either the original image or the place and the people photographed.[25]

Recognising that images are socially constructed, how, then, do we respond to Jacob A. Riis's belief that his photographs of the poor demonstrated that 'The power of fact is the mightiest lever of this or any day'?[26] His crime-reporting in New York City concentrated upon the individual tragedies brought about, or at least exacerbated, by poverty and slum conditions. But his landscapes are contrived to appear shocking not to stir up the people to seize power, but to stir the compassion (or fear) of people in authority, such as the President of the New York Police Board (and later New York Governor), Theodore Roosevelt. Through lecture tours across the nation, Riis warned the propertied classes to change these conditions before it was too late. His pictures were deliberately meant to shock, to stir, to frighten. His pictures might present facts, but his message was a product of his times. Lewis W. Hine, however, was more self-aware of his craft, recognising that his selection of the dross from industrial society was deliberate and didactic, encouraging the viewer to be less a voyeur than a witness to such degeneration.[27]

Washington DC: the growth of a national capital

The nineteenth century saw cities grow at an unprecedented rate, within minimal constitutional ground rules. Strategic decisions to create western garrisons or to enact tariffs that favoured certain ports over others provided no guidelines for the management of these turn-of-the-century cities. The pressing need to maintain order, provide services, and co-ordinate expansion on such a novel scale was far more problematic than state legal codes alone could handle. The Census Bureau's gathering of information gave an impetus to city promotion and subsequent growth. Free delivery in rural areas enabled mail-order catalogues to widen the bounds of US consumer culture, thereby helping to create a more standardised landscape, whether parlour decor inside, or screens, porches and flag-poles outside. The US Commerce Department started to encourage research and development by the building industry; its support for building codes increasingly influenced the changing urban landscape. The US postal service also had a considerable impact upon the urban fabric when it insisted upon the existence of certain neighbourhood standards, such as street signs, house numbering and the provision of sidewalks, before it would start regular deliveries. But this was all piecemeal. The planning and early execution of the national capital at the beginning of the nineteenth century, however, influenced layout design and set the style for public buildings throughout the USA. As the layout of the capital was designed to demonstrate and reinforce specific political relationships, while also expressing the dominant ideology of the new republic, its development had wide repercussions.

In the London of the previous century, the architect Inigo Jones had already sought to create a suitable capital for the supposed magnificence of Stuart rule, calling upon the most advanced architectural theories. Any attempt to create such 'total architecture' was, however, far more likely to be successful, albeit for republican aims, on a new American site than in London, where piecemeal redevelopment left room only for specific, individual buildings, however grandiose. In a new, purpose-built federal district on the shores of the Potomac, rules of perspective could be placed at the disposal of democracy, not made a means of reducing urban landscapes to a personal statement of royal control. Indeed, the original L'Enfant plan (named after the first architect), though much modified, remains indicative of that particular ideological view of the world from which it emerged, an urban version of Jefferson's western frontier. Like the ideal, Utopian cities conceived during the Italian Renaissance, Washington DC was to be an architectural totality with a perfect and, therefore, changeless form, reflecting the triumph of republicanism.[28] The separation of powers, that core doctrine of the US constitution, was built into the very fabric of the city: at its most obvious, the White House and the Capitol are at opposite ends of Pennsylvania Avenue.[29] From the White House it may seem that all roads (both the typical US grid and the local addition of radial avenues) lead to the presidential mansion, placing the President at centre stage. From Congress, however, there is an even more obvious centrality: not only do the streets and avenues focus upon Capitol Hill, so too does the street-numbering system. This congressional view is reinforced by an unparalleled view westwards (that most American of directions) which encompasses the Mall, a wide and grassy expanse, with its array of national shrines to Presidents Washington, Jefferson and Lincoln. This central axis was to be no thoroughfare, but a public open space, the simple formalism of which would give the new heart of the capital a garden-like feel, as befitted an agrarian republic.

The key governmental and administrative buildings were situated around the Mall. Significantly, the Supreme Court building was not located to create a symbolic grand triangle with the White House and the Capitol, suggesting that the judiciary was not initially seen as the equal of the two elected branches of government. The layout was to suit neither aristocrats nor merchants, but representatives, ennobled by the tasks and responsibilities conferred upon them by their constituents. A modern cynic might think that the architectural impression of so much monumental architecture is more conducive to ennobling administrators than representatives.

As in typical townscape paintings of the Italian Renaissance, the buildings of the republic's government would rise in dignified symmetry, the converging perspective drawing the eye across an opulent and humanised landscape under a serene sky, a suitable prospect for a once idealised and now realised world of order and harmony, quite at odds with the chaos of Old World cities and the dockside mayhem of American ports. The pure line, the human scale, and the proportional symmetry of Renaissance classicism, once available only to the few, could now, in the New World, be made available to the newer democratic notions of citizenship. The overall impression of the observer set down within this environment was to be of a rationally established administrative and legislative order, appropriate for the capital of a rational republic. There was no room here for the confusion of medieval-type streets, as in old Boston, nor for the complex geometry of papal Rome, its opera-like intricacies epitomising its baffling rituals and appeals to the senses rather than to reason. Republicanism should be sustained through logic and clarity, not mystification and complexity.

The grid plan was borrowed from Philadelphia, city of brotherly love, and the great intersecting avenues were named after the various states. Pennsylvania Avenue would have a central role, linking the executive and legislative modes, as befitted the 'keystone' state. Where the avenues and grid streets intersected, there would be fifteen urban nodes, one for each member state. Today these are mostly roundabouts, often the only ones that most Americans ever have to negotiate in a nation otherwise wedded to the traffic light-controlled right-angled intersection. It was to be many years, however, before the plans produced anything more striking than an overgrown village. In the early 1830s Mrs Trollope was impressed by 'the appearance of a metropolis rising gradually into life', though, only eighteen years later, Charles Dickens was disappointed with the 'spacious avenues that begin in nothing and lead to nowhere'. Prospects were not encouraging: 'Take the worst part of Pentonville ... Burn it down, build it up again in wood and plaster, widen it a little ... plough up all the roads ... plant coarse turf where it ought *not* to be, erect three handsome buildings ... make it scorching hot ... and that's Washington. Such is it likely to remain.'[30] Strict adherence to the original L'Enfant plan seems to have been abandoned. The Mall became cluttered and incoherent (in architectural parlance), while in-filling had removed the Potomac River (and an associated canal) from active involvement in the life of the city. The original plan called for a statue of George Washington at the intersection of the lines of sight from the White House southwards and the Capitol eastwards, on a site that overlooked the river. Instead, the statue became a high memorial obelisk, built off-centre (for technical reasons) and completed only in 1884.

The Macmillan Commission (with landscape architects such as F. L. Olmsted, Jr. previously associated with the grandiose Chicago Columbian Exposition in 1893) decided to complete the conversion of the Mall from an infinite, open landscape appropriate for an expanding republic to an enclosed architectural composition (walled in by monuments or public buildings) more fitting for a post-frontier USA. So today the heart of the capital is a transported and enlarged formal garden, surrounded, like the villa gardens of antiquity, by statues, porticoes and buildings within planned but ultimately contained perspectives. Subsequent buildings, at least in the downtown Federal Triangle and adjacent overspill areas, have tended to continue the use of adopted classical forms. The new republic increasingly saw itself as a new Rome for a New World. The first half of this century saw the urban landscape expressing the US cult of size, as the American republic, in competition with Britain in particular, revelled in a bigger land mass, a larger population, and an increasingly grand capital. The National Archives and the Supreme Court buildings both resemble great classical temples, though their scale tended to become colossal rather than human. There was an emphasis upon the suprahuman in this new grandeur, where architecture and landscape would dominate and, thus, intimidate the individual. Even the democratic impulses behind the New Deal seemed to result in administrative buildings dangerously akin in scale and heroic decoration to socialist realism, if not Nazi celebration of one people, one land.[31]

The L'Enfant plan dealt with only part of the federal district. Today it can be seen as the inner city bounded by Florida Avenue, where the modern city streets start to climb away from the swampy lands of Foggy Bottom. Here the 'Federal Triangle' still reflects the city's primary purpose: government. Large federal agencies are housed in neo-classical buildings, many dating from the expansion of the federal government's role in the New Deal era. The city's central commercial area is poorly developed – not just because most retail business is now conducted in shopping malls out in the Maryland and Virginia suburbs, but because the city's retailing and commerce has always been that of a medium-sized southern town rather than a northern city. There is little regional or national commerce, banking or manufacturing (unlike its equivalent-sized neighbour, Baltimore, only thirty miles away). Instead, the offices of lobbyists, lawyers and the media fill the wide avenues that radiate from the White House. Uncharacteristically, these buildings, whether ultra-modern or restored, are restricted in height so that none can overlook the Capitol. Beyond the federal district, there is no wider continuation of the capital's planned pedigree; rather, the expanding suburbs involve a landscape of freeways, shopping malls, business parks and entertainment complexes, plus associated housing tracts. These archetypal post-war suburbs boomed in the Reagan years, when speculative post-modern projects sprang up along the new interstate highway from the Langley headquarters of the CIA westwards to Dulles International Airport.[32] The various contrasting ages and styles of suburban architecture display the various eras within which this development has taken place. Garret Park, Maryland, was a former dormitory suburb for commuters working in the district of Columbia; its ageing housing stock just over the DC line stands in contrast to the larger, more modern homes further out along the arterial roads that the commuters of the 1950s and 1960s used. Further out still, newer stock reflects the building booms geared to the beltway, the interstate highway around the whole metropolitan area which consolidated suburban pre-eminence over the inner city and, despite the building of an underground railway system in the 1970s to link selected parts of suburbia with the central city, dispersed commuters and shoppers over a diffused suburban landscape, linked together by roads and the electronic media.

Notes

1. See Robert F. Looney, *Old Philadelphia in Early Photographs 1839–1914* (Dover: New York, 1976). Similar volumes exist for Washington DC and for New York City.

2. Oliver Jensen *et al.* (eds), *American Album* (American Heritage: New York, 1968).

3. David Harvey, *The Condition of Postmodernity: An Enquiry into the Origins of Cultural Change* (Basil Blackwell: Oxford, 1989).

4. Mike Davis, *City of Quartz: Excavating the Future of Los Angeles* (Verso: New York, 1990), and Edward E. Soja, *Postmodern Geographies* (Verso: New York, 1989), both explore these themes within southern California.

5. Jean Gottman, *Megalopolis* (20th Century Fund: New York, 1961), is a classic. For

an update, see David Clark, *Post Industrial America: A Geographic Perspective* (Methuen: London, 1984).

6. Joseph S. Wood, '"Build, Therefore, Your Own World": The New England Village as Settlement Ideal', *Annals of the Association of American Geographers* 81 (1991), pp. 32–50.

7. John P. Radford, 'Race, Residence, and Ideology: Charleston, South Carolina in the Mid-Nineteenth Century', *Journal of Historical Geography* 2 (1976), pp. 329–46, reprinted in David Ward (ed.), *Geographic Perspectives on America's Past* (Oxford UP: New York, 1979).

8. Richard C. Ward, *The Urban Frontier: Pioneer Life in Early Pittsburgh, Cincinnati, Lexington, Louisville and St Louis* (University of Chicago Press: Chicago, 1959), can usefully be read in conjunction with Mrs Frances Trollope, *Domestic Manners of the Americans* (1832; reprinted by Alan Sutton: Gloucester, 1984).

9. The classic study is Sam Bass Warner, *Streetcar Suburbs: The Process of Growth in Boston (1870–1900)* (Harvard UP: Cambridge, Mass., 1978). For a wider exploration, try Kenneth T. Jackson, *Crabgrass Frontier: The Suburbanization of the United States* (Oxford UP: New York, 1985).

10. David R. Meyer, 'The New Industrial Order', In Michael Conzen (ed.), *The Making of the American Landscape* (Unwin Hyman: Boston, Mass., 1990), pp. 249–68, and Edward K. Miller, 'The Americanization of the City, *ibid.*, pp. 269–92.

11. Michael P. Conzen, 'The Progress of American urbanism, 1860–1930', in Robert D. Mitchell and Paul A. Groves (eds), *North America: The Changing Geography of a Changing Continent* (Hutchinson: London, 1987), pp. 346–70.

12. David Ward, *Cities and Immigrants* (Oxford UP: New York, 1971), explores the relationship between expanding central business districts and adjacent ethnic neighbourhoods.

13. Peter O. Muller, *The Outer City: Geographical Consequences of the Urbanization of the Suburbs* (Resource Paper No. 75/2, Association of American Geographers, 1976).

14. Jane Jacobs, *The Death and Life of Great American Cities: The Failure of Town Planning* (Penguin: Harmondsworth, 1965).

15. Sharun Zukin, *Landscapes of Power: From Detroit to Disney World* (University of California Press: Berkeley, 1991), places the Detroit case study within wider concerns, particularly the interplay between market economics and the cultural dynamics of a market-based society.

16. Harvey, *The Condition of Postmodernity*, pp. 66–98, deals extensively with the Baltimore situation.

17. Margaret Crawford, 'The World in a Shopping Mall, in Michael Sorkin (ed.), *Variations on a Theme Park: A New American City and the End of Public Space* (Noonday: New York, 1992), pp. 3–30, uses Canada's West Edmonton Mall to explore this phenomenon in a most accessible and provocative essay. By extension, the same points apply to the more recent Mall of America in Minnesota and to all further clones.

18. Bass Warner, *Streetcar Suburbs*.

19. Donald A. Mackay, *The Building of Manhattan* (Harper and Row: New York, 1987), is a brilliantly illustrated, vertigo-creating exposition of the technical side of skyscraper construction. For more pedestrian approaches, see R. Banham, *Megastructures: Urban Futures and the Recent Past* (Harper and Row: New York, 1976), or D. M. Reynolds, *The Architecture of New York City* (Macmillan: New York, 1984).

20. See Mary Black, *Old New York in Early Photographs* (Dover: New York, 1973).

21. Alan Trachtenberg, *The Statue of Liberty* (Allen Lane: London, 1976), explores the pedigree and construction of the statue, with one final chapter on its iconic role within US society.

22. John A. Jakle, 'The Metropolis as an Attraction', in *The Tourist: Travels in Twentieth-Century North America* (University of Nebraska Press: Lincoln, 1985), deals with the skyline as an urban icon.

23. Alan Trachtenberg, *Brooklyn Bridge: Fact and Symbol* (University of Chicago Press: Chicago, 1979), does to the bridge in the background of so many movies and television shows what he had done earlier to the Statue of Liberty.

24. Richard Lacayo and George Russell, *Eyewitness: 150 years of Photojournalism* (Little Brown: New York, 1990).

25. Mick Gidley, *American Photography* (British Association for American Studies Pamphlet No. 12, 1983), provides an excellent introduction to this.

26. Jacob A. Riis, *The Making of an American* (1900), ed. Roy Lubove (Scribner's: New York, 1966). For good or ill, Riis, like Hogarth and Dickens in Britain, helped to define our images of the 'lower orders' and their surroundings.

27. Alan Trachtenberg *et al.*, *America and Lewis Hine: Photographs, 1904–1940* (Aperture: Millerton, NY, 1977).

28. John Reps, *Makings of Urban America: A History of City Planning in the United States* (Princeton UP: Princeton, NJ, 1963), and *Monumental Washington: The Planning and Development of the Capital Center* (Princeton UP: Princeton, NJ, 1976).

29. As Denis Cosgrove, *Social Formation and Symbolic Landscape* (Croom Helm: London, 1984), points out: 'The ideal city is designed for the exercise of administration and justice, for the civic life, rather than for production or exchange. It is purely ideological' (p. 94).

30. Marc Pachter (ed.), *Abroad in America: Visitors to the New Nation 1776–1914* (Addison-Wesley: Reading, Mass., 1976), explores the reactions of these and other visitors to the new republic. Cities such as Washington DC soon became, along with Niagara Falls, essential to any well-conducted tour. The contrast between the best-laid plans and the realities is explored in Frederick Gutheim, *The Federal City: Plans and Realities* (Smithsonian Institute Press: Washington DC, 1976).

31. J. Valerie Fifer, 'Washington DC: The Political Geography of a Federal Capital', *Journal of American Studies* 15/1 (1981), pp. 5–26.

32. Robert A. Harper, 'Metropolitan Washington: Center of an Interconnected Network', in *Between Two Worlds* (Houghton Mifflin: Boston, 1973), pp. 2–27, deals with the city just before an era of massive growth; see also Paul L. Knox, 'The Restless Urban Landscape: Economic and Sociocultural Change and the Transformation of Metropolitan Washington, DC', *Annals of the Association of American Geographers* 81/2 (June 1991), pp. 181–209.

CHAPTER 6

Studying the Urban Landscape

As the previous chapter has shown, Washington DC remains unusual, in that its core was comprehensively planned and laid out. Most cityscapes are the product of previous decisions and later adjustments over many generations.[1] Whether constructed piecemeal or by grand design, any cityscape must exist upon and within a pre-existing landscape. Suburban Long Island still shows the previous outlines of farms, for the land was bought from developers piecemeal, utilising – and rarely ignoring – existing property lines. The mid-western grid pattern can be picked out across the Chicago suburbs, for again it was agricultural land that was bought and built upon. Sometimes even Indian and colonial routes can still be discerned within the modern metropolis – as where Broadway cuts across Manhattan's grid pattern, for example, from the site of Dutch 'Nieuw Amsterdam' south of Wall Street up to 'Haarlem' on the Hudson. Cityscapes, then, can be valuable clues to social, political and economic relationships not immediately apparent otherwise. Why do some features survive and others disappear? What drives changes in the suburban landscape?

Different types of expansion between one city and another may indicate not just contrasts in prevailing aesthetic taste, but varying degrees of involvement in wider economic changes. The rapid growth of suburbia in post-war Washington DC has a lot to do with a recession-proof local economy geared to a rapidly expanding federal government, with its myriad agencies, private consultancies and lobby groups. The massive growth of specific suburban nodes such as Tyson's Corner reflects not just the popularity of certain post-modern styles with architects and clients alike, but the promotion of a particularly credit-driven boom which resulted in the largest ever US budget deficit. Why certain areas within actively redeveloping cities have remained intact while others have been changed out of recognition is hotly debated.[2] A wide range of studies demonstrate the various ways in which urban actors can exploit a city's opportunities, lifting the constraints of location and power to leave their impact upon the city. Few works study the urban landscape for its own sake, yet work in urban geography,[3] architectural history,[4] and political economy[5] illustrate how such landscapes can be read as documents, teasing out the way in which the individual parts were created and the totality put together.

As the USA has moved beyond industrialisation, novel structural realignments may initially be most apparent within the landscape. Whereas social changes are often difficult to monitor, massive changes within the built environment can be remarkably evident not just to the academic, planner or politician, but to the average citizen or visitor. Over the last twenty years, the corridor of development that now links central Washington DC with Dulles International Airport in northern Virginia is a widely recognised reflection of more fundamental changes within metropolitan society. Other areas have also undergone massive de-industrialisation, factory closures and urban decay. Some, such as Lowell, Massachusetts, have subsequently been redeveloped, with high-tech businesses being shoe-horned into former industrial premises. Such a range of changes, mostly within the urban arena, suggest that industrial society has been radically transformed – if not completely, then at least substantially – all across urban America, within the northern 'Snowbelt' as much as within the silicon valleys of the Sunbelt.

The decline of manufacturing and the concomitant rise of service-sector employment is characterised in the growth of 'edge cities' – business and science parks, and retail complexes (malls) – reflecting the new locational and land-use requirements of post-industrial society. Social commentators have seen the growth of such service and high-tech industries in terms of the emergence of a new middle class, perhaps most evident in the historic preservation and gentrification of downtown districts such as Back Bay in Boston or Georgetown in Washington DC.

Change and transition are normal in the US landscape. The American urban landscape is restless, reflecting alternating periods of prosperity and economic recession (boom and bust) along with large-scale unemployment (particularly amongst certain groups), most evident in the inner city. Even if a stable post-industrial society were to emerge, which looks increasingly unlikely, the landscape will always contain elements of the past. Even overtly post-industrial areas are embedded within far older arrays of landscape elements: 'a traveller to an American city ... encounters an urban landscape that proclaims its newness alongside the vestiges of its past. New in the landscape presents a dynamic image, while "old" represents hindrance.'[6] But this has been true since the late nineteenth century. Is post-industrial society so radically different that radically new landscapes are now emerging?

Technology continues as the symbol for change, though gigantism has been overtaken by images of miniaturisation, mass production by value-added, and a centralised population by one ever more decentral-ised. At the heart of this transition has been the decline of manufacturing and the rise of economies geared to the provision of services. The abandonment of traditional industrial areas in parallel with the develop-ment of urban fringes has been one of the most remarkable changes in the landscape since the 1940s and it has taken place on an unprecedented scale. A decline in the importance of manufacturing has forced large numbers of manufacturers to invest in huge new enterprise zones and science parks along the freeways and near the airports rather than to reinvest in existing cramped inner-city sites. Few firms actually migrate from inner-city sites; rather, the inner-city firms decline, with new firms likely to be created elsewhere. Even rationalisation and mergers have had profound implications for inner-city economies and, therefore, for inner-city work forces, making the urban industrial landscapes of the last two hundred years less and less relevant today. The overall negative impacts of decline have, to some extent, been counteracted by commercial and industrial expansion both in new areas and within expanding suburbs, but the local impact can be devastating. Landscape degradation often is the most obvious sign of inner-city decline, particularly for passers-by.

The emerging post-industrial landscapes reflect lower employment densities, flexible production and the pursuit of economies of scope rather than scale; these reflect local economic restructuring following challenges to the economic regime of mass production and mass con-sumption that was so associated with Henry Ford.[7] The suburbanisation of businesses and people is said to be the most important trend in shaping the contemporary landscape. Suburbanisation and decentralisation have been the result of the accelerated obsolescence and multiple disincentives of the inner city, including high land prices, low-quality housing, un-reliable public services and rising crime levels. Almost two generations of 'white flight' to the suburbs has had a profound impact upon American city centres as the suburban exodus relegated central neighbourhoods to minority and low-income groups, particularly African Americans and recent immigrants trapped by federal welfare and housing programmes in those parts of the city where the demand for labour was increasingly depressed. The downtown image became one not of dynamism, but of minority pedestrians, government-service workers, and all-weather shoppers.[8]

Corporate offices that were once considered the bastions of the city, such as the major firms listed in *Fortune Magazine*, increasingly transferred their headquarters from the largest metropolitan areas, including New York, which had to fight back with ever more spectacular redevelopment projects to enhance or even replace images of the traditional downtown. The growth of high-tech industry, particularly computer software, biotechnology, pharmaceuticals and research and development, has had a major impact in shaping the new post-industrial landscape. New high-tech industries require a highly skilled, highly educated and flexible workforce. Many high-tech industries cannot find acceptable locations even in the old industrial cities which do not suffer from the image of a degraded environment and an unskilled, inflexible and often militant workforce; the computer firm Wang wanted to find a greenfield site in Boston with access both to downtown commercial and university skills and to the national freeway network. Such footloose enterprises have novel locational requirements; they can dictate to local areas or look elsewhere at other edge cities, business parks and high-technology corridors.

The expansion of the service and high-tech industries, with its inherent requirement for highly educated and skilled employees, has led to the growth of a new bourgeoisie, with specific consumer patterns removed from the vulgarity of mass consumption to a concern for niche markets.[9]

Changing patterns of consumption mean that retailers have had to move beyond the provision of a limited range, with its call to 'stack it high and sell it cheap', set within purely functional surroundings. Consumers want a shopping experience, with recycling areas, coffee shops, and even entertainment; some of the new malls have not just multiplex cinemas, but also mini-theme parks for the children. Shopping has become a family day out, with forgotten items bought subsequently from 24-hour stores, usually adjacent to or within petrol stations. Breaking away from the functional architecture of the post-war period means that the post-modern landscape often includes bizarre mixes of down-market functional facilities alongside post-modern buildings copying well-known regional or ethnic styles and next to buildings which are deliberately eye-catching in their unusualness – where an entrance seems like a collapsed wall, for instance, or the top of building is finished off like a massive carving.

During the 1950s and 1960s, cityscapes were increasingly geared to the needs of traffic rather than pedestrians: 'one by one skyscrapers come to turn impersonal wall of stone and glass to sidewalks little used'.[10] The spending power of the new middle-class consumer, however, has meant some reversal of this trend as new shopping malls go some way towards redressing this imbalance: cars are still necessary to get there and to take purchases away, but they are generally kept outside, whether in downtown convention centres or edge-city complexes.[11] This reinforces the growing trend to produce a set of structures that are not generally accessible to the public except as they arrive as potential shoppers, as consumers rather than residents. This is an increasingly privatised world from which undesirable groups can be excluded – both in that there is nothing specifically provided for them and in that modern security systems will identify and exclude those who do not fit in. Imagine bringing a group of young black teenagers into a modern shopping mall as part of a course in the geography of retailing; get them to stand around while you explain traffic flows to them; then stand back and watch the arrival of very nervous security guards, alerted by video cameras whose operators report on any gatherings or on the presence of 'undesirables'. Walkways within malls are not public rights of way, but private land, over which potential customers are allowed to pass at the developer's discretion. The street has become a factory-style space.

The contemporary landscape has come to reflect the imperatives and attitudes of modern post-industrial North America. Urban areas have seen a renewal of interest in old and quaint buildings, which have become the subject of historic preservation: 'a self-conscious and selective revival of elements of older styles, and this is exactly what has been happening in revitalisation, preservation and urban design'.[12] Old factories have been renovated into shops and condominium apartments in almost every city. Along the restored Chesapeake and Ohio Canal in the Georgetown section of Washington DC, once derelict factories have been gutted and transformed into shopping centres, a form of commercial gentrification which matches what had already happened to neighbouring housing. Old buildings and old districts such as north Boston are no longer regarded as obsolete or a hindrance to planning, but invaluable components of the contemporary landscape, providing a suitable ambience with which to attract those who, in another generation, had fled to the suburbs.

The modern American city exhibits a complex set of landscape elements. Just as the traditional pattern of immigrant neighbourhoods around a prosperous central business district evolved into a depressed black inner city around an ageing central business district surrounded by expanding white suburbs, so the urban landscape also continues to change. It is ever more fragmented, with competing shopping and service centres, as the black middle class move out into once white suburbs, as childless white middle-class couples move into inner-city redevelopments, and as edge cities continue to attract most of the area's incoming investment. Transition has become the norm within this modern landscape as social, cultural and economic imperatives make themselves manifest. The notion that the urban landscapes of the great northern cities, such as industrial Chicago, are the norms towards which other towns gradually develop becomes increasingly irrelevant. Not only are newer cities such as Phoenix unconstrained by such industrial-era layouts, but even the older cities are being restructured to resemble these new cities – if only to compete for incoming investment. While this may seem to suggest that a terrible 'sameness' is creeping over the land, the context within which these modernising developments take place are so different that nationwide homogeneity is unlikely. The cultural context of an increasingly Mexican Los Angeles is quite different from that of the far more diverse New York City, which in turn is a world away from that of mid-western Minneapolis; Pittsburgh's massive changes have revitalised the city in ways quite unlike those pertaining in Detroit, which has never recovered from the end of the Ford-era mass production upon which black and white workers alike relied.

Notes

1. There would seem to be strong echoes here of Karl Marx's assertion that 'men make their own history, but they do not make it just as they choose [being limited by] circumstances directly encountered, given and transmitted from the past': *Eighteenth Brumaire of Louis Napoleon* in Marx and Engels, *Selected Works* (Foreign Language Publishing House: Moscow, 1935), p. 247. In making cities, people are, of course, making their own history.

2. W. E. Firey, *Land Use in Central Boston* (Harvard UP: Cambridge, Mass., 1947), argues that such was the sentimental attachment of older, affluent, and politically active residents to certain parts of the inner city that developers sought easier targets, where the poor and inarticulate could be moved out easily. Susan Fainstien's work in Manhattan, New York City in the late 1980s confirms that similar interaction between power and sentiment remains a vital aspect of urban change.

3. Kevin R. Cox and R. J. Johnston (eds), *Conflict, Politics and the Urban Scene* (Longman: Harlow, 1982).

4. Tom Wolfe, *From Bauhaus to Our House* (Farrar, Straus, Giroux: New York, 1981), is an irreverent guide. For a more traditional but well-illustrated introduction, see Lucy Peel, Polly Powell and Alexander Garrett, *An Introduction to 20th Century Architecture* (Apple Press: London, 1989). For the national capital, see Warren J. Cox *et al.*, *A Guide to the Architecture of Washington, D.C.* (McGraw-Hill: New York, 1974).

5. Michael N. Danielson and James W. Doig, *New York: The Politics of Regional Development* (University of California Press: Berkeley, 1982).

6. Edward K. Muller, 'Distinctive Downtown', *Geographical Magazine* (October 1980), p. 747.

7. Paul L. Knox, 'The Resless Urban Landscape', *Annals of the Association of American Geographers* 81/2 (June 1991), pp. 181–209.

8. Muller, 'Distinctive Downtown', p. 753.

9. What Knox ('The Restless Urban Landscape') sees as a shift from the ' "vulgar functionalism" of modernist mass consumption' to post-modernity's 'aestheticized commodity', with connotations concerned with status, chic and wit.

10. John A. Jakle, 'Landscape Redesigned for the Automobile' in Michael Conzen (ed.), *The Making of the American Landscape* (Unwin Hyman: Boston, Mass., 1990), pp. 293–310.

11. E. Relph, *The Modern Urban Landscape* (Croom Helm: London, 1987), p. 257.

12. *Ibid.*, p. 213.

CHAPTER 7

Theme Parks and
Heritage Landscapes

Washington DC is not America's only planned community. There has been a long history of planned communities, from Shaker villages, via comprehensively designed new towns such as Columbia, Maryland, and Reston, Virginia, to the spread of hippie communes in the 1960s. Corporations have built company towns for their workforce, the most famous being Pullman in suburban Chicago. And, after World War Two, massive suburban communities such as Levittown, Pennsylvania, were built by private housing developers. Of interest here, however, are two kinds of planned landscapes that are generally under-represented in landscape studies: theme parks [1] and heritage sites, two increasingly popular sites which, while different in many ways, nevertheless exhibit remarkably similar characteristics.

Theme parks are not as ephemeral as might initially be thought. Amusement parks such as New York's Coney Island have a long history, constituting important landscape elements in the expanding cities of the industrialising nineteenth century. [2] Within the massive suburbanisation of the 1950s, however, something new emerged: Disneyland. Here was a new kind of quasi-public space that sought to harness the popular appeal of amusement parks while avoiding their less attractive, down-market aspects. As a development deliberately placed beyond the existing urban landscape of Los Angeles, Disneyland was to have a massive impact locally and, increasingly, nationally and internationally. By the early 1970s, Disney World had been opened in a vast estate, an integrated network of parks which has utterly changed central Florida.

Theme parks differ from amusement parks in many crucial ways, not least of which is the fact that they occupy a contained and clearly delineated, usually rather large, site. Unlike seaside resorts such as the Atlantic City boardwalk, visitors cannot wander in and out at will, spending as much or as little as they choose. Payment is made up front, in exchange for unlimited access during a designated length of time.

With the contemporary prevalence of credit cards, with their deferred repayments, a large initial outlay is not quite the disincentive that it might otherwise seem. Furthermore, visiting a theme park is usually planned, involving family members who are excited about their forthcoming treat, so price resistance at the point of payment is minimised. In addition, Disney World cunningly gets people on to the site, through the parking area and on to the lake ferry long before they appreciate the expense of a family package. Few, by then, are going to turn around and walk away. The layout of the park has been designed to draw people in; furthermore, it is already familiar even to the new visitor. Two generations of children have been brought up with Disney movies, products and television. Not only is product promotion aimed at moving vast amounts of merchandise, but its very familiarity makes the vast site less threatening than might first appear. Many families feel that they are visiting familiar territory, from which they can then branch out into unknown areas, such as the various foreign exhibits around EPCOT (Experimental Prototype City of Tomorrow). Like the world fairs, all the world seems to be on hand at Disney, to be accessed without threat or expense.[3] A British pub is as accessible as a Norwegian church. In such synthetic surroundings, the ultimate virtual reality helps to create and then reinforce certain American images not just about the USA, but about the wider world and, by inference, America's place within that world.[4]

The Magic Kingdom lies at the core of all Disney theme parks. Main Street USA has been widely recognised as reflecting the array of attitudes towards the urban past that were epitomised in folk memories of the Midwest at the end of the nineteenth century, including ambivalent attitudes towards both technology and commerce.[5] The community that is being celebrated is that which was undermined by the arrival of mass production, mass culture, and mass consumption, the very aspects of modern society within which Disney theme parks are most securely located. However, no irony is recognised in what is little more than a parody of real main streets: shopping is reduced to trinkets and fast food, traffic is scarce and reduced to replica classic vehicles. Despite the small-town claims, nobody actually knows your name.[6] The perspective of upper floors is manipulated to make the view seem 'more real', or at least more cosy. Parades take place at least twice a day, not twice a year. And not only are there no horse droppings, but there is no garbage, at least not for long. Cleaning up is prompt and maintenance takes place after hours. The world of work has disappeared – ironic, given the value given to honest hard work within mainstream American culture. Beyond Main Street, there are themed areas focusing upon other places and other times, whether foreign or mythical (though these are often confused).[7] Rides are usually based around Disney movies, such as the Peter Pan, or are generic representations of places that have been created by the movies, such as Pirates of the Caribbean. Technology has long been a major theme, with an area within the Magic Kingdom specifically dedicated to portraying the future. Technology has now been given its own site, at least in Florida, where EPCOT provides an eye-catching, almost iconic, sphere within which technology is portrayed as the saviour of the planet. From a visitor base initially reliant upon young adults with young children, Disney theme parks have widened their appeal to include all ages, from gentle sightseeing cruises through a virtual Norway to white-knuckle rides such as Space Mountain, with parades and fireworks for all ages. Such elements have now become so standard that their presence on rival sites is deemed, by the general public, to be an essential part of a theme park.[8]

But the impact has not just been in terms of theme-park sites and their environs. So successful has Disney been in promoting a new type of site that Disneyland and its offshoots have become the yardsticks for an ever wider range of facilities for the general public, from motorway service areas and shopping malls, by way of world fairs and convention centres, to galleries and museums.[9] Detractors may abhor the ubiquity of Disney products, but the significance of Disney probably has more to do with its influence on this range of modern facilities. Every shopping mall developer, not just every amusement park operator, has to respond to the way in which Disney has set the tone and the pace for large, integrated site developments. Just as Ford set standards in the factories, so Disney sets standards in consumer facilities. And, with this, come other cultural values that are encoded into the very landscape. Disneyland and Disney World both depend upon and confirm the primacy of the car (in the US sites, though not necessarily abroad, given the different roles of the railway networks in France and Japan). More importantly, such large facilities ignore the previous landscapes. The site is treated as virgin wilderness. This is no inner-city facility which, however modern, has to be squeezed into a pre-existing street pattern and made compatible with its neighbours. The old landscapes are completely obliterated, whereupon the site acts as a honey-pot, attracting other similar and complementary facilities, such as hotel and tourist facilities. In creating jobs, this stimulates growth in the local housing market, thereby promoting a further population influx and making it necessary to provide a growing range of public facilities such as schools and police stations. Both Disneyland and Disney World are surrounded by rival parks offering different themes, such as Sea World in Orlando. An expanding landscape comes to be seen as a normal, healthy landscape, without reference to a growing environmental impact that may not be sustainable. Disneyland has been partly responsible for a massive suburban expansion on the edge of what is really a desert, and Disney World has spawned even more expansion in an area which, though not desert, is using up underground fresh water faster than nature can replenish it.[10]

While it might seem that many of these features are merely unintended consequences of Disney's initial need for an unusually large site, it is worth recalling that Disney himself was concerned to resist New Deal attitudes that were urban, immigrant, and north-east based. In southern California he could help to build another vision of the post-war world, one which, while having echoes of the mid-western small town, grew out of the massive wartime influx of predominantly young people from all over the USA, people who would visit his facility in family groups. Thus Disneyland would reflect the more constrained atmosphere of the world fair and escape the blighting factors that had long since undermined New York's Coney Island, with its bawdy fairground atmosphere, unchaperoned young people, and immigrants coming in on the subway. Later, in Florida, Disney was further to exemplify the world fair, when he proposed to inaugurate EPCOT, though this never progressed beyond being an extension of the corporate stands so prevalent at world fairs. Instead of enabling people to live in an experimental urban setting, as originally envisaged by Walt Disney himself, the corporation retreated to a position as a showcase for American technology after his death. Recently, however, the corporation has returned to urban concerns with the inauguration of Celebration, a town built and run by the corporation. This new town, adjacent to the Disney compound, is designed to distil the lessons of supposedly successful towns such as Charleston and Savannah in order to re-establish small-town America, though cynics might suggest that this is a corporate attempt to broaden the Florida portfolio to include real-estate development. Even initially unsympathetic journalists and critics have noted the high standard of facilities, however, and the sophisticated ways of managing public expectations. These are aspects that have had a considerable impact on other complexes that deal with the general public, even those that would normally be appalled to have anything to do with theme parks, such as art galleries and museums. But it is within open-air museums and other similar heritage sites that the often subtle influence of Disney can be found.

Despite the growing impact of Disney theme parks, most landscapes emerge from the rough interplay of inertia and redevelopment on an almost *ad hoc* basis; even where indicative planning has become part of this interplay between owners, developers and government, certain landscapes have been designated as special and, therefore, outside American society's normal assumption that change is the norm. Such landscapes are deemed shrines, worthy of being preserved and visited – not always a happy conjunction. Such valued landscapes are no longer restricted to the far western wilderness, or even their eastern equivalents. Battle-fields, early settlement sites, buildings characteristic of a particular epoch, all are valued beyond any immediate economic value, and visited for their cultural significance rather than for any immediate contribution to daily survival.

However, public images of America's past never quite escape the mythic power of the West. On a par with the Manhattan skyline, Monument Valley and the Grand Canyon sustain belief in the sublime nature of the American experience as made visible in such spectacular wilderness. Images of President Reagan as a rancher highlight a western experience that can still be seen in films as varied as *Fifel Goes West* (1990) to *Unforgiven* (1992), while the French computer game *Alone in the Dark 3* (1995) sets its frontier adventure in the Navajo lands of Arizona. Even such supposedly revisionist occasions as 'The West as America' exhibition at the Smithsonian Museum in Washington DC, or the movie *Dances with Wolves* (1990), challenged prevailing orthodoxy even while remaining essentially concerned with the lands beyond the Mississippi. With a resurgence of western environmentalism, an increasingly Hispanic south-west, and the growing importance of Pacific Rim issues, public interest remains focused upon the West of today rather than that of the colonial period. Though Frederick Jackson Turner's claim that only westward expansion explains the American experience has long been rejected by scholars, recent attempts to reach beyond the academic community to a wider public still detract from the cultural importance of earlier, eastern frontiers.[11] It is not that academics have ignored the West of the early English speakers; rather, this is considered colonial rather than frontier history. Mention the frontier and people envisage Fort Apache rather than Jamestown's stockade. But it was in eastern areas that Americans developed ways of creating landscapes that were geared to eliminating the native peoples in favour of staple crops and long-distance trade. Just as the origins of the republic lie in eastern experiences, so, too, eastern landscape transformations are at the root of the development of an American landscape experience. And it is back east that Americans now locate 'heritage landscapes'. In attempting to locate the origins of frontier landscapes in the east, however, museums and heritage sites encounter problems inherent in the presentation and representation of such a disputed past within the landscape of today. The landscapes of the colonial seaboard were geared to imperialism, slavery and environmental exploitation. Did not Thomas Jefferson transform British imperialism into an 'Empire for Freedom', where decadent traditions would find no root? It is in eastern landscapes that modern Americans would find traces of both their colonial past and of their revolutionary struggle towards independence – rival, if not contradictory, elements of American heritage. What transforms particular places into heritage sites? Which particular sites come to be revered? Must the commemoration of US independence and the Civil War overwhelm all heritage landscapes? It is crucial to understand which past is preserved, re-created and presented, for it is in such landscape images, rather than in scholarly tomes, that the general public, who have little interest in the concerns and caveats of professional historians, are most likely to come into contact with the explicit traces of colonial and early national landscapes, those sites that commemorate the very foundation of the republic and, as shrines, are central to America's myth of origin. As Salman Rushdie (1989) reminds us: 'What America loves most, needs most ... is the myth of itself.' [12]

Eastern states are well supplied with sites that focus upon early settlement.[13] The two best-known are Plimoth Plantation in Massachusetts and the Jamestown Settlement in Tidewater Virginia. Seeking to commemorate and yet demythologise aspects of the early colonial frontier, both sites present replicas of the initial English fortified settlements. Both sites are scrupulously researched re-creations adjacent to the original historical sites,[14] using a landscape form to expand the democratic practices enshrined at the Smithsonian Museum in Washington DC in its collection, display and commemoration of the commonplace. Such shrines to ordinary life provide visitors with objects to be contemplated for their wider, democratic and, therefore, American significance. It is as if Copeland's *Fanfare for the Common Man* has been built into the very fabric of landscapes central to the American sense of identity. The buildings chosen for display in such sites are deemed exemplary, an array of landscape elements seen as central to understanding the way in which America came into being. Both sites use replica landscapes to locate American experiences within a wider tapestry, that of the 'English-speaking world'.

The open-air museum expands the nineteenth-century technique of placing individual pieces of furniture, traditionally ones associated with the great and the good, within the context of a fitted-out period room. The period room is then relocated within an appropriately re-created building, within an array of similar buildings, to create – by accident or, increasingly, by design – a synthetic landscape. Such replicas never-theless appear reminiscent of the ethnographic displays that emerged as essential exhibits within the great imperial expositions [15] and, more recently, those arch-promoters of 'reckless eclecticism', theme parks. [16] Open-air museums may not have the economic impact of theme parks, [17] but they play a vital role in actively reproducing cultural images of particular people, places and periods; once such images have been popularised, they become difficult to challenge. [18] But a paradox emerges at the very moment that such landscapes seem most real and natural. The very act of ordering a sequence of buildings, particularly juxtapos-ing and omitting certain buildings, fixes a particular set of historical relationships, those approved by the curators, in landscape form. The more real the appearance, the more the site presents a specific amalgam of what is deemed worth visiting. This has more in common with a literary canon, an array of books that will enlighten and that, supposedly, represent the best that the culture can provide, than with a normal everyday landscape, which is usually an array of varying degrees of disorder, from the suburban strip of fast food and car lots to the Man-hattan skyline. Heritage sites are spatial experiences deliberately engineered from a plan, even if that plan is to preserve certain battlefield vistas and not others, to encourage visitors to explore here, but not there, or to create sufficient replicas to enable modern visitors to envisage the site in previous times, such as during a battle, such as at Manassas, south-west of Washington DC, or a siege, such as Yorktown in the Virginia Tidewater. Given that popular culture has helped to create a common visual vocabulary, specific, powerful triggers (such as flags, cabins and wagons for frontier landscapes; flags, guns and ditches for battles and sieges) are deliberately enhanced to encourage specific, almost visceral, reactions from visitors.[19] Curators are well aware of the evocative power of wood smoke in transporting visitors across time, in experiencing a past that existed before the complexities of the modern world cut us off from such simple pleasures. Heritage landscapes, even more than particular artefacts, are peculiarly effective in suggesting that the very authenticity of their exhibits confirm the myths being commemorated. Unlike paintings and photographs, landscapes imply that they are not images, but an unmediated reality – life as it really is, rather than a virtual reality.

But do such replica landscapes allow the public to recognise that the presentation is a theatrical stage, created on top of, or adjacent to, an original landscape? Would the casual visitor recognise that such heritage landscapes are the product of conflicts and tensions between various interest groups, each of which probably wanted to highlight a different theme? Curators wanted to do this, the accountants that, and consultant academics something else. What emerges is necessarily a compromise, as is the case within any commercial enterprise. But whereas a theme park does not claim to be offering the public an authentic glimpse of a lost world in 'Pirates of the Caribbean',[20] open-air museums do just that. The problematic aspects inherent in any representation of the past remain occluded from public perception in favour of images that are supposed to show 'how things really were'. To reinforce this stance, heritage sites emphasise their academic rather than their tourist credentials.[21] Despite rhetorical claims to be time machines, heritage landscapes are not neutral windows on a lost world. Rather, they reflect the complexities of the social and cultural disagreement involved in their establishment and maintenance. Guidebooks from the 1950s suggest that the seventeenth century then was a very different place than it is today!

The Yorktown siege and British surrender sites illustrate a paradox about such developments: should visitors be shown what is most authentic or what is most spectacular? There were two distinct eras during which Yorktown was surrounded by earthworks: the War of Independence and the Civil War, eighty years later. Important Civil War battlefields are two a penny across Virginia, and nothing much actually happened in Yorktown during the Civil War. Defensive ditches were dug to protect a town whose control might turn the fate of the South, as had been the case in the previous conflict. Older, Revolutionary War ditches were dug out, reused and, in helping to deflect Union activity elsewhere, did what was required of them. But, in so doing, the earlier battlefield landscapes were severely disrupted, over and beyond the normal ravages of time. Today, however, many of the ditches have not only been dug out again for the visitor, but the Civil War ditches are used, where necessary, to stand in for the earlier ones.[22] Whereas minor Civil War sites clutter the South, there is only one site for the final British surrender at the end of the War of Independence. This is obviously the occasion that this site should commemorate. So the fiction is maintained (in all but a small, out-of-the-way panel within a museum gallery) that the landscape being presented is that of the Revolutionary, rather than the Civil War, siegeworks. What the visitors want is what is provided. In the process, however, heritage landscapes become something quite complex, as concerned to promote cultural myths as to educate the visitor, even though these landscape are ostensibly committed to providing authentic, rather than mythical, views of the past.

Research suggests that visitors respond to open-air museums in terms of their overall effect rather than as a series of individual displays.[23] Folk parks generally offer pre-industrial heritage landscapes by way of a series of authenticated, though relocated, buildings and their contents.[24] They are quite different from, but closely resemble, restored sites such as Williamsburg, where a decayed colonial town has been rebuilt *in situ*. Here are replicated the buildings that had previously existed together on that very site. Whether brought together from across a cultural region or restored on site, such reconstructions preserve, share and, indeed, create public memory.[25] As repositories of memory, however, whose memory do they preserve? As snapshots of time, reconstructions such as Old Sturbridge village can all too easily convey an ahistorical nostalgia for a golden age,[26] particularly at seasonal events such as Thanksgiving. The Museum of American Frontier History in Staunton, Virginia, brings together buildings, plus immediate surroundings, from both sides of the Atlantic. On a site lacking specific importance, the authenticity of relocated exhibits is everything. Thus distinguished from a theme park such as Old Dominion, with its 'Olde Worlde' areas like 'Bonny Scotland', the open-air folk museum offers a glimpse of the past,[27] seemingly unmediated and unadulterated by the misconceptions and myth-making of popular culture. In both what they present and ignore, however, such heritage sites embody the tastes, attitudes and dynamism of their – usually, liberal-minded – creators. Uneasy with issues of class or race or religion, heritage sites favour the presentation of images of integrated communities.[28] Like all museums, they demonstrate an almost Victorian belief that material culture, both as individual artefacts and together, as landscapes, can represent fundamental aspects of the human experience, and that the clutter of the past can be presented in a comprehensible manner. The only issue is how to install and maintain the most efficacious presentation. There is no place here for post-modernist exhibits that might suggest that the past was an incomprehensible, or merely confusing, cacophony of warring interests. The Whig view of history prevails: the visitor only has to look at the site to see how far we have progressed.

The creation of any single assembly of buildings to typify the USA, the South, or a particular period has not gone unchallenged,[29] so museums that are not entirely site-dependent often create settings that tell a story, a narrative validated by authenticated items. Change can be introduced to a degree that is not possible in museums offering a the 'day-in-the-life' snapshot, whether before emigration (as at the various ancestral homes of US Presidents and other worthies found across Ireland) or after immigration (as at Rocky Mount, Tennessee).[30] Whereas the replica American landscapes at the Ulster American Folk Park stand in deliberate contrast to their pre-emigration exhibits, its sister museum in Staunton, Virginia, presents an array of carefully authenticated, relocated buildings from Germany, Ireland and England[31] which are explored along a circuit that leads to a relocated 'American' farm. In so doing, Staunton seemingly follows the requirement of the International Committee for Archaeological Heritage Management that 'Presentation and information should be conceived as a popular interpretation of the current state of knowledge, and ... be revised frequently',[32] for newly arrived buildings are brought to life using the latest reconstruction and presentation techniques. However, Staunton does not challenge visitors' preconceptions through exposure to *new* scholarship. Whereas some museums seek to trigger personal memories, helping visitors to link biography with history[33] (Ellis Island in New York harbour, or the US Holocaust Memorial Museum in Washington DC), something else is evoked within frontier museums.[34] Artefacts are chosen in terms of their ability to trigger folk reminiscences rather than family memories, with no recognition of inevitable deformations or manipulations. Replicas and reconstructions invite visitors to mistake the artefacts for the events that they represent. Though such a critique is commonplace to literary scholars, museums pride themselves on following the codes of professional historians, geared to empirical verification rather than semiotic decoding, which they may well consider little more than pretentious whimsy. If the historical process generated particular buildings, which we then use to represent frontier life, then artefacts are being asked to act as traces, even relics, rather than as metaphors. Heritage sites have, indeed, become shrines. But physical fragments are inert lumps of matter – until deemed important, when they become signs wherever and however displayed. How much more so when they are relocated, repositioned, or amalgamated with other buildings and contents in arrangements never previously extant.[35] Such buildings are then given a privileged status, confirming an empirical connection between a past situation (the frontier experience) and a present experience (being an American), even when discontinuities between artefacts are elided and when the landscape amalgam that is created is totally synthetic.

Moving through such artificial landscapes element by element compresses a long historical process into the physical experience of the visitor. But the story is a simple algorithm – follow the line of reasoning, and the end point, understanding, is assured. Staunton believes that it offers a problem: how did these various foreign traditions become part of an American heritage?[36] Given the deeply held popular belief in the efficacy and desirability of the melting-pot, however, the visitor already knows the answer. The Old–New World pathway reinforces an existing framework of understanding via the statement of a particular, unchallenged view of America's past, a white, Anglo-Saxon Protestant perspective worthy of the Buffalo World's Fair of 1901.[37] Furthermore, the Staunton narrative sustains the popular view of a staid, unchanging and, thus, repressive Europe. The American frontier is deemed to be the only place where Europeans could break with such a past-ridden present and forge their own futures. An array of changeless European landscapes is needed if the US is to appear altogether novel. Seeing the frontier as but an extension overseas of English and Scottish settlement in Ireland,[38] would suggest not uniqueness, but continuity.

Open-air museums such as Staunton install synthetic heritage landscapes between fact and illusion through the presentation of simulated realities, plausible through unreal. The more coherent the narrative, the more visitors are willing to suspend their disbelief, albeit in a circuit around a landscape that confirms a particular museum's own theme, such as the myth of America's frontier origins. At Staunton, emigration is deemed to stimulate cultural change (evident in new artefacts, epitomised by the American farm) even while accepting that identities such as English, Ulster or American [39] are as definitively fixed as the seemingly timeless Old World buildings on display. Buildings seem real rather than shifting cultural signs. Such cultural categories are, however, highly problematic: the plasticity of memory is matched only by the fluidity of supposedly fixed ethnic elements.[40] And why are such venues unwilling to present unsettling or problematic aspects of their theme? As places where visitors are encouraged to enjoy their cocoonment within a changeless world, perhaps such self-contained landscapes have become 'a kind of escapism, a flight from the uncertainties of the present to the apparent stabilities of the past'? [41] Any substantive presence of the outsider and the dispossessed, or concern for the problematic relationship between artefacts and cultural change, would inhibit escapism. Is this the origin of the paradoxical and unintended resemblance to theme parks? [42] As elsewhere, the outsider, the 'other', has generally been eliminated, excluded, or assimilated within acceptable images. At Jamestown, Pocahontas, in statue form, has become an Old World Cinderella.[43] No wonder a Disney movie was later to resurrect her as an American Founding Mother.

How do American heritage sites respond to the New World's indigenous peoples? Though the native core of American culture is ever more apparent across the USA, the *significant* outsider in Jamestown and Plimoth remains the British, an 'other' that can readily be grasped as part of a common transatlantic culture, an otherness with whom Americans still share fundamental values. Aboriginal peoples are problematic within such a strategy; their presence at sites of settler pilgrimage is idiosyncratic. Native peoples are not kith and kin. To ignore them, however, is to perpetuate the nostalgic notion that America was essentially a land open and empty, ripe and ready, when European peoples arrived.[44] Both the Virginia and the Massachusetts sites do at least provide indigenous encampments, some otherness within the dominant group's shrine. The same can *not* be said about Virginia's interior sites, where the native peoples seem all too often never to have existed. Settlers moving into the Shenandoah Valley did find what, to them, seemed empty and inviting landscapes;[45] by the beginning of the nineteenth century, the native peoples were indeed almost totally indistinguishable in lifestyle from their neighbours.[46] But the commitment

of Staunton's Museum of American Frontier Culture to a particular
notion of the frontier (the famous Turner thesis) effectively compounds
traditional white views of native peoples as exotic asides or pathetic
footnotes; it does not see the native experience as part of 'a mutual
history of continuous interaction and influence'.[47] Indeed, the New
World may differ from the Old World precisely to the degree that
interaction between settlers and indigenous people has been crucial,
even where it is not immediately apparent. Cultural historians now
maintain that, without an indigenous presence, American identity as we
know it today would not exist.[48] More specifically, a true appreciation
of what the frontier actually looked like requires a native presence.
In the Shenandoah Valley, however, heritage landscapes ignore non-
European contributions. Nowhere in the Staunton landscape is there
any recognition that the Shenandoah Valley was not, in the eighteenth
century, awaiting its first human footprint. Nor would visitors at any
other of the folk museums along the Shenandoah (such as Crab Orchard
and Rocky Mount) realise that this was a contested landscape. Without
an awareness of an indigenous presence along the Virginia frontier, we
can have no sense of specifically American rather than transplanted
European dimensions – ironic, given that the Staunton museum is not
the US Museum of European Folk Architecture, but the Museum of
American Frontier Culture.

George Eliot's novel *Adam Bede* (1859) opens by inviting the reader
into a workshop 'as it appeared on the 18th of June, in the year of Our
Lord, 1799'. By a neat rhetorical trick, a realistic illusion, the reader is
invited to enter a scrupulously delineated, historically authenticated
narrative in circumstances that would otherwise remain hidden from
view. Eliot's strategy paralleled that employed by the British landscape
artist Joseph Wright in his painting *An Iron Forge Viewed from Without*,
where one wall is cut away to allow the viewer to glimpse what would
normally remain hidden inside, a technique itself borrowed from hydro-
logical diagrams that laid bare the hidden workings of pipes, valves and
drains.[49] Just as fiction and painting, in letting scenes tell the story,
pretend that there is no author, only a reader or viewer, so heritage
landscapes consist of a series of set pieces that carry the visitor forward
on a narrative which inhibits any awareness that what is being presented
is an authored and, thus, mediated experience. Folk parks select buildings
which substantiate their non-theme park status while confirming a particular thesis about the past. Thus, heritage landscapes only superficially

meet historians' criteria for accuracy, internal consistency, and congruence with the surviving record. An honest recognition of landscapes as rhetoric, of the disputed nature of this approach, with a suitable 'name and a place' [50] for the excluded and enslaved peoples is surely appropriate. Without stating publicly that museums still impose an authoritative voice upon a disputed past, such preferred narratives remain wedded to mythologies hardly different from those of imperial expositions or theme parks. Disneyland and Disney World are at least honest in treating the past as simply a ride. Or do they?

Notes

1. Stephen F. Mills, 'The Contemporary Theme Park and its Victorian Pedigree', in Stephen F. Mills and Steve Ickringill (eds), *Victorianism in the United States: Its Era and Its Legacy* (VU Press: Amsterdam, 1992), pp. 78–96.
2. John F. Kasson, *Amusing the Million* (Hill and Wang: New York, 1978).
3. Paul Greenhalgh, *Ephemeral Vistas: The Expositions Universelles, Great Exhibitions and World Fairs, 1851–1939* (Manchester: Manchester UP, 1988).
4. Stephen F. Mills, 'Disney and the Promotion of Synthetic Worlds', *American Studies International* XXVIII/2 (October 1990), pp. 66–79.
5. Richard Francaviglia, 'Main Street USA: A Comparison/Contrast in Streetscapes in Disneyland and Walt Disney World', *Journal of Popular Culture* 15 (1981), pp. 141–56.
6. The television series *Cheers* makes much of its theme tune's 'Where everybody knows your name', small-town virtues in an inner-city bar. But in the real Boston bar used on the show's credits, nobody knows your name, for it is now a tourist trap, a replica of a mythical re-creation of a neighbourhood bar – pure Disney.
7. D. M. Johnson, 'Disney World as Structure and Symbol: Re-Creation of the American Experience', *Journal of Popular Culture*, Summer 1981, pp. 157–65.
8. E. W. and J. Mechling, 'The Sale of Two Cities: A Semiotic Comparison of Disneyland with Marriott's Great America', *Journal of Popular Culture*, Summer 1981, pp. 166–79.
9. M. Sorkin (ed.), 'See you in Disneyland', in *Variations on a Theme Park: The New American City and the End of Public Space* (Hill and Wang: New York, 1992), pp. 205–32.
10. A. Wilson, *The Culture of Nature: North American Landscape from Disney to the Exxon Valdez* (Blackwell: Oxford, 1992), provides an interesting environmental context within which to consider Disney theme parks.
11. Patricia Nelson Limerick, *The Legacy of Conquest: The Unbroken Past of the American West* (Oxford UP: New York, 1987).
12. Reviewing E. L. Doctorow, *Billy Bathgate*, in *The Observer*, 10 September 1989.
13. Though, of course, the first Europeans to arrive in the present territory of the USA were Spanish, in the present south-west and Florida.
14. Barnum, in his Disney reincarnation, still haunts such accessible museums, in that they are afraid of being mistaken for theme parks. As commodification blurs boundaries, it is small wonder that the International Committee for Archaeological Heritage Management seeks to re-establish categories by emphasising authenticity

through 'qualified professionals', 'expertise' and 'postgraduate training programmes' (Charter: Article 8): *Antiquity* 64 (1993), pp. 402–5.

15. Donald Horne, *The Great Museum: The Re-presentation of History* (Pluto: London, 1984); Mills, 'The Contemporary Theme Park and its Victorian Pedigree'.

16. Chris Rojek, *Ways of Escape: Modern Transformations in Leisure and Travel* (Macmillan: London, 1993), and Stephen F. Mills, 'Disney and the Promotion of Synthetic Worlds', *American Studies International* 28 (1990), pp. 66–79.

17. Though this should not be underestimated, if such facilities are part of a wider tourist portfolio. In the Virginia Tidewater, where each heritage site, whether Jamestown, Williamsburg or Yorktown, is an essential element in the region's growing visitor appeal.

18. Robert Hewison, *The Heritage Industry* (Methuen: London, 1987).

19. Andrew Sherratt, 'Archaeology and Post-Textuality', *Antiquity* 67 (1993), p. 195, discusses using images rather than words.

20. Though this distinction may be disappearing as EPCOT, following its status as a permanent world fair, offers more and more foreign exhibits or glimpses of technological change.

21. Emphasising that their staff hold PhDs rather than MBAs, that they sponsor conferences rather than hold conventions, and that they generally promote scholarship rather than profitability.

22. This is not a uniquely American issue. The finest stretches of England's World Heritage Site, Hadrian's Wall (as seen incongruously in *Robin Hood, Prince of Thieves*), are strictly Victorian restorations rather than what has survived intact, the latter being far less spectacular.

23. Nick Merriman, 'Museum Visiting as a Cultural Phenomenon', in Peter Vergo (ed.), *The New Museology* (Reaction Books: London, 1989), pp. 149–219.

24. Kenneth Hudson, *Museums of Influence* (Cambridge UP: Cambridge, 1987), pp. 113–43.

25. James E. Young, 'The Texture of Memory: Holocaust Memorials and Meanings', in *Writing and Rewriting the Holocaust: Narrative and the Consequences of Interpretation* (Indiana UP: Bloomington, 1988), pp. 172–206.

26. Lawrence Keeley, *Myth of a Peaceful Savage* (Oxford UP: New York, 1985), suggests that despairing academics seek refuge in folk memories of more tranquil times.

27. Jay Anderson, *Time Machines: The World of Living History* (American Association for State and Local History: Nashville, 1984).

28. Alan Gailey, 'Creating Ulster's Folk Museum', *Ulster Folklife* 32 (1986), pp. 54–77; David Brett, 'The Construction of Heritage', in Barbara O'Connor and Michael Cronin (eds), *Tourism in Ireland: A Critical Analysis* (Cork University Press: Cork, 1993), pp. 183–202.

29. Critics see them as history theme parks; see Philip Norman, *The Eighties, the Age of Parody* (Hamish Hamilton: London, 1990).

30. With its re-creation of the day that the first territorial governor arrived in 1794.

31. The first English farm was actually a replica of a listed building that could not be removed from the UK.

32. 'Article 7: Presentation, Information, Reconstruction', reprinted in *Antiquity* 64 (1993), pp. 402–5.

33. James E. Young, 'Holocaust Memorials: The Politics of Identity', in William Frankel (ed.), *Survey of Jewish Affairs 1991* (Blackwell: Oxford, 1992), pp. 161–73.

34. David Lowenthal, 'Pioneer Museums', in Warren Leon and Roy Rosenzweig (eds), *History Museums in the United States* (University of Illinois Press: Urbana, 1989), pp. 115–27.

35. Hence the ICAHM Charter's expectation (Articles 3 and 6) that preservation and interpretation should happen *in situ.*

36. Young, 'Holocaust Memorials', p. 164: 'As a land of immigrants the [Holocaust] survivors had hoped America would also be a land for immigrants' memories, of pasts that are "foreign" only in so far as they transpired in other lands, but American in that they constitute the reason for having to come to America in the first place.'

37. Robert W. Rydell, *All the World's a Fair* (University of Chicago Press: Chicago, 1984).

38. Raised inside Jamestown's museum, though not alluded to outside.

39. Werner Sollors, *The Invention of Ethnicity* (Oxford UP: New York, 1989), pp. xiv–xv.

40. Liam Kennedy, 'Ethnic Memory and American History', *Borderlines* 1 (1993), pp. 130–41.

41. Raphael Samuels, 'People's History', in *People's History and Socialist Theory* (Routledge: London, 1981), p. xxxiii.

42. Gary Wills, *Reagan's America* (Heinemann: London, 1987), explores 'declawing' the past within venues such as theme parks.

43. Robert S. Tilton, *The Pocahontas Narrative in Antebellum America* (Cambridge UP: Cambridge, 1994). Pocahontas has been put to multiple, often contradictory, uses in miscegenation, racial conflict, and colonial expansion debates.

44. William M. Denevan, 'The Pristine Myth: The Landscape of the Americas in 1492', *Annals of the Association of American Geographers* 82 (1993), pp. 369–85.

45. Robert D. Mitchell, 'The Shenandoah Valley Frontier', *Annals of the Association of American Geographers* 62 (1972), pp. 461–86.

46. Theodore W. Allen, *The Invention of the White Race* (Verso: London, 1994), parallels the experiences of indigenous peoples in Virginia and Ireland.

47. James Axtell, 'Colonial America without the Indians: Counterfactual Reflections', *Journal of American History* 73 (1987), pp. 981–96.

48. *Ibid.*

49. See Judy Egerton, *Wright of Derby* (Tate Gallery: London, 1990), pp. 103–4.

50. From the Hebrew *Yad Vashem*, providing a marker for those individuals and communities that were destroyed in the Holocaust.

Conclusion: American Studies and the American Landscape

This study has focused upon the look of the land, with only an occasional concern for those other traditional strengths of the geographical imagination, regional identity and a sensitivity to the patterns and flows of social and economic life. My intention has been to extend the horizons of readers for whom landscape may appear to be an ephemeral, if not irrelevant, aspect of American Studies. I have suggested that a concern for the American landscape is a concern for the cultures that have moulded it, providing a vantage point from which the workings of society can be examined, if not in all their complexities, at least in a fresh light.

Landscapes have traditionally been analysed from two radically differing perspectives: that of the complex artefact that is the built environment, long explored by geographers and architectural historians; and the image, a perspective associated with both the artist and the critic. This study has suggested that not only are both traditions necessarily partial, but that each can gain from an awareness of the other's perspective. The American environment is not just the product of human processes, lacking all cultural dimensions or implications. For something to be built, it had first to be imagined. People learned what to expect from earlier experiences of other landscapes, whether overseas or back east. Many reacted against their experiences and sought to build radically new surroundings, while others attempted to re-create familiar features, producing, in the nature of things, a partial copy, demonstrating both its pedigree and its novelty. In much the same way images of the landscape reflect not just an artistic pedigree, the subject of so much art history, but also the concerns of the day. The architect Mies van der Rohe used to point out that 'Architecture is the translation of its epoch into space.'[1] So is it with all buildings, as well as with the space between them, even if this is not always immediately apparent. America is a composite creation of past and present, of the moulding of the environment by individuals and groups – sometimes deliberately, sometimes as the unintended result of other activities.

Recognising such complexities, landscape analysis has moved on to use approaches developed in other cultural fields. The avowedly atheoretical approaches that dominated landscape studies for many years failed to address adequately which elements of the landscape (or, better still, what combinations of elements) are significant and, therefore, worth studying. Without adequate theoretical concerns, analysis is rudimentary, restricted to locating, describing and tracing the histories of artefacts within the landscape. This is a necessary starting-point, perhaps, but a superficial goal. The stance of 'record just what you see' is naïve, for what you see is conditioned by what you anticipate.[2] Even if landscapes could be considered organic rather than the products of human activity, they are not self-contained. They are products of social processes and power relationships; just as life and society have many divergent, even conflicting, meanings, landscapes, too, are capable of multiple meanings.[3] Inhabited landscapes are cultural productions – that is, systems of meaning. Even where they are self-evidently agencies of food production, such as the mid-western corn belt, or industry, such as the area around the Great Lakes, the meanings of landscapes are neither self-evident nor unproblematic. People value them for other reasons, which could be seen when the Navajo resisted departure from their traditional lands, south of the Grand Canyon, or when Appalachia's people stayed on in worn-out mountain hollows. Where literary texts are seen to have changing and multiple readings (often quite divorced from the author's own intentions), so, too, landscapes are seen not just as a series of Freudian slips which occasionally let the cat out of the bag, but ways in which people and groups talk to each other. Landscapes can be seen as arenas of competing discourses, operating at various levels. Just as processions have a rhetorical element, so landscapes are implicitly, sometimes explicitly, designed to make a statement. Few Americans could miss the Confederate message of Georgia's Stone Mountain, where southern heroes have been carved out of the rock. Whatever statements are expressed in the landscape of Atlanta's wider metropolitan area are more complex to discern.

So, contemporary landscape analysis starts with a series of questions rather than an opening salvo of mapping or data-recording. How does this particular landscape encode information? How does this landscape help or impede particular cultural (social, political or economic) practices? How important is the landscape in making cultural statements: a necessary, integral or sufficient part? How does this landscape present, or make visible, aspects of the culture that otherwise would lie hidden or forgotten? Does this landscape act as a repository of memory? Does it remind people of who they are? Does it empower them or inhibit them? How are recollections of the past emphasised in the landscape, and for whose benefit? Though such questions can be applied most obviously to a planned city, like Washington DC, they can be applied just as easily to less comprehensively assembled landscapes. Did the southern plantation landscape enhance white control and inhibit black resistance? Do those elements of this historical landscape that survive today also empower the white population and inhibit black empowerment? Or is today's southern landscape redundant in such matters, even while indicted in their creation? Why does Virginia revere the landscapes associated with its defeated armies? Answers may be both more complex and more interesting when dealing with vernacular landscapes, where multiple authorship means a far greater interplay of competing elements, than in more overtly authored landscapes, such as those of Pullman's company town or Disney's theme parks.

Does the study of the US landscape provide a peculiar entry into what makes America different? Can the outsider ever experience the USA vicariously, through an appreciation of the landscape images with which we are so familiar? The framing of the landscape painting or photograph or movie sequence clearly places the viewer outside the frame. Can this distance only be removed by stepping into the place itself, by visiting the USA? Is it necessary to step back into the frame by becoming an inhabitant? At least the landscape would not be experienced vicariously, but by living and working within it. Academic dichotomies such as image and reality, people and surroundings, would collapse, or at least become irrelevant, within the essential, experiential unity of living. The landscape would cease to be a partial glimpse, but an experience of the flow of history. We would no longer be removed, alienated, from the landscape, and thus would be more fully human. It is just this kind of argument that has led scholars such as J. B. Jackson to focus upon individual dwellings as the primary landscape element, with a concern for the vernacular at the heart of any interest in the landscape. Only here, the argument goes, can we (the outsider or visitor) hope to see the fundamentally democratic and populist leanings of Americans. Perhaps the problem lies in landscape being beyond the formal approaches of scholarly or intellectual control, needing to be experienced rather than considered. And this, too, though highly debatable, is a very American way of responding to the world about us: don't just talk, do it.

Even a cursory glance at the modern, particularly metropolitan, landscape will reveal a wealth of juxtaposed, incongruous landscape elements. There has been no comprehensible grand plan. The postmodern rejection of any single vantage point, any single grand theory, has been very attractive in recent landscape studies, for the tensions that exist between classes, races and power groups in society not only mirror the complexities of landscape, but legitimise the realisation that an organic landscape (as sought by early landscape students, such as Carl Sauer) cannot possibly exist. Even where there have been attempts to create unified, organic landscapes, as in the case of Mormon Utah or L'Enfant's Washington DC, internal and outside pressures alike have caused radical deviation from such supposedly timeless norms. Postmodern concerns have encouraged a concern for landscapes' differences, whether the widespread product of general processes, locally unique, but explicable in terms of an interaction between general processes, or singular, uniquely distinctive and remarkable to the degree that no general statements can be made about them.

As time and space are increasingly compressed within electronically interconnected and commercially homogenised interstate landscapes, the combination of active and relict features within the landscape makes for an ever more complex set of surroundings, the built environment and its representations. This complexity itself encourages academic and media attempts to simplify our understanding of it, suggesting models and stereotypes with which Americans can make sense, or otherwise, of their surroundings. Both academic and media simplifications involve decoding and deconstructing landscape features, inevitably re-encoding and reconstructing our responses to landscape. This may not necessarily involve seeing the modern city as a 'soft city',[4] totally malleable and amenable to personal manipulation to specific private needs, but it certainly goes far beyond the notion that cityscapes are either immutable, deterministic structures which control our lives or, alternatively, are irrelevant, transparent figments of our imagination, having no significant impact upon a USA of individualistic mores, winners and losers, frontiers and the space race.

But how far can we go in seeing landscapes as texts written in the language of the concrete – views made apparent? How far do sets of architectural features and their location convey allegorical information, reinforcing certain beliefs, aspirations or ways of life? How do the grand schemes, whether created incrementally or comprehensively, influence the interactions between power relations and everyday life? How do Americans subvert their surroundings? How do they subvert other people's images of what their landscape should be? It might initially appear that those who are dominant within the power structure create environments which simply enhance, or at least reinforce, their own dominance. In their ordinary everyday lives, however, people have an amazing propensity for subverting the best-laid schemes of those in power. The growing study of the vernacular landscape suggests that any critical reading of the American environment which deals only with people's image of their surroundings or with the power relations that constrain them, while ignoring their everyday, actual use of landscape, will remain necessarily partial.[5]

So, this brings us back to the perennial question: does what makes the USA different from other societies reside, to some degree, in its landscape? Certainly, few other countries have been so successful in presenting landscape images for others to fear or enjoy. Having this sense of expectation so geared to images of the USA means that the real America frequently comes as a surprise to the first-time visitor, particularly when the familiar landscape feels so strange, like the foreign country that it really is, after all.

Notes

1. See Charles Knevitt, *Space on Earth* (Methuen: London, 1995), p. 94.
2. The Carl Sauer school of cultural geography and the W. G. Hoskins school of local history nevertheless both did essential ground-breaking work. Hoskins's *The Making of the English Landscape* (Penguin: Harmondsworth, 1955; rev. 1976) remains a classic, though strangely parochial in scope, and is essential reading for any student of the landscape in North America. See D. W. Meinig, 'Reading the Landscape: An Appreciation of W. G. Hoskins and J. B. Jackson', in D. W. Meinig (ed.), *The Interpretation of Ordinary Landscapes* (Oxford UP: New York, 1979).
3. Paul Coones, 'One Landscape or Many? A Geographical Perspective', *Landscape History* 7 (1985), pp. 5–12.
4. Jonathan Raban, *Soft City* (Hamish Hamilton: London, 1974).
5. Allen Pred, *Journal of Historical Geography* 17/1 (1991), p. 117, a review of James S. Duncan, *The City as Text* (Cambridge UP: Cambridge, 1990).

Suggestions for
Further Reading

Despite the best efforts of the Landscape Research Group in the UK and the journal *Landscape* in the USA, there is no formalised discipline of landscape studies, with its own methodologies and university departments. In the absence of any organisational or disciplinary unity, landscape studies all too often consist of a great variety of unrelated perspectives, tied only loosely to the environment and its representation. For the beginner (or the teacher, seeking to offer the enquiring student some direction within an unfamiliar field), this lack of an obvious formalised focus can be infuriating and then off-putting. Though a growing number of titles do offer 'landscape' on the cover, many will be a disappointment: the term has become a catch-phrase to sell books, almost irrespective of their content.[1] Considerable patience may be necessary to identify books that actually deal with landscape evolution or landscape images. Despite the recent expansion of explicitly landscape texts, analysis of both landscape history and landscape imagery is often buried within other titles. There is no convenient, all-encompassing slot and no single library classification. Much relevant research is considered to be cultural geography or local history, but might equally well be found within archaeology or art history rather than landscape analysis. Much material is buried within discussions on social and economic change, merely one of the unintended consequences of historical development. Recent books on regional geography usually turn out to be more concerned with systematic issues (such as transport networks, economic development and social problems) than with landscapes as such. Indeed, landscape analyses are now found under such a wide range of headings – archaeology, architecture, economic history, cultural geography, historical geography or regional studies – that even those students who continue to assume that their central theme is merely the description and interpretation of the human imprint upon the physical environment will find that even this, somewhat limited, perspective will no longer save them from exploring an ever-growing breadth of sources. Add the vast literature from the visual arts tradition, and the potential scope widens to encompass a plethora of material on paintings, photography, and the mass media. This inability to contain landscape studies within a straightforward academic framework, however, is more than a matter of finding widely scattered secondary sources, but an indication of its interdisciplinary breadth, emphasising its potential for American Studies.

Texts that focus specifically upon the US landscape have, until recently, been very difficult to obtain, especially in Europe. Many landscape papers have been submerged within a wide range of US journals, and even such US texts as Christopher Salter's *The Cultural Landscape* (Duxbury: Belmont, CA, 1971) contains only one or two overtly landscape chapters, its title notwithstanding. It could just as equally have been called 'A Reader in Human Geography'. Wilbur Zelinsky's *The Cultural Geography of the United States* (Prentice-Hall: Englewood Cliffs, NJ, 1973) was too densely written for outsiders without first-hand experience of the concerns of US geographers and the USA itself. Recently, though, publishers have come to recognise that there is a market for texts dealing explicitly with the landscape, so access to first-class secondary material is at last becoming possible. No course of study would be complete now without recourse to D. W. Meinig (ed.), *Interpreting Ordinary Landscapes* (Oxford UP: New York, 1979), and Michael Conzen (ed.), *The Making of the American Landscape* (Unwin Hyman: Boston, 1990; now available through Thompson in the UK). Though the latter text echoes W. G. Hoskins's classic text, *The Making of the English Landscape* (Hodder and Stoughton: London, 1955), the US volume lacks a single voice, nor, despite the landscape painting on the cover, does it deal with landscape images: a crucial loss, for, like its namesake, it ignores half of the landscape equation. For most European students, the study of US landscapes is necessarily vicarious, producing a curious paradox. While US landscapes are probably the most widely recognised around the world, and many Europeans feel more familiar with a USA that they have not actually visited than with their own continent, US landscapes are still remarkably inaccessible to most people, even Americans. The aim of this final section is to encourage those who are interested in American culture to consider landscape studies as a viable and vital aspect of American Studies and to bring a wide range of printed materials to their attention. Major texts and material on substantive issues are highlighted for those anxious to broaden cultural studies away from our present over-reliance upon film, television and popular music, however vital these traditional aspects may be. In so doing, the concerns of many historical and cultural geographers may emerge as having much to offer cultural studies in general and Americanists in particular.

The very term 'landscape' is used, confusingly, in many different ways. For many writers, it still seems to apply only to specific landmarks to be saved from destruction.[2] On the other hand, geographers often fail to consider landscape *per se* amidst the wealth of detail on river flows, electrification and regional revitalisation: the Tennessee Valley Authority being seen as a dream come true for the International Federation of Landscape Architects![3] Fortunately, others, particularly cultural geographers, increasingly use the term as a holistic, or at least heuristic, device, allowing them to cross traditional disciplinary boundaries to discuss features that would otherwise be seen as discrete rather than interacting. Some seek to understand the landscape itself, others to use it as a novel way of exploring the societies of which it is an outward and visible sign.

It has long been realised that people respond to their perception of their surroundings rather than to any 'objective' situation. How this 'perceptual environment' is created, sustained, and sometimes even challenged has been of considerable interest to geographers, urbanists and particularly psychologists. *Mental Maps*, by Peter Gould and Rodney White (Penguin: Harmondsworth, 1974), combines these three perspectives. For a historical example, see Louis de Vorsey, 'The New Land: The Discovery and Exploration of the Eastern North America', in Robert D. Mitchell and Paul A. Groves (eds), *North America* (Hutchinson: London, 1987), pp. 25–47. A new, massively revised edition of this is due out soon and is eagerly awaited. Useful review articles can be found in L. J. Wood, 'Perception Studies in Geography', *Transactions of the Institute of British Geographers* 50 (1976), pp. 129–42. The recognition that people respond to what they think is going on around them has been particularly fruitful for understanding the way in which people respond to hazardous environments and, by extension, to the natural world in general. Clarence J. Glacken's *Traces of the Rhodian Shore: Nature and Culture in Western Thought from Ancient Times to the End of the Eighteenth Century* (University of California Press: Berkeley, 1976) is a classic exploration of the interaction between nature and culture.

The attitudes of different cultural groups can be explored in Yi-Fu Tuan's *Topophilia: A Study of Environmental Perception, Attitudes, and Values* (Prentice Hall: Englewood Cliffs, NJ, 1974). This can be followed up in his essay 'Geopiety: A Theme in Man's Attachment to Nature and to Place', in David Lowenthal and Martin Bowden (eds), *Geographies of the Mind* (Oxford University Press: New York, 1976), and in *Landscapes of Fear* (Pantheon: New York, 1976). There is, however, a rival stance: that environmental perception – indeed, landscape aesthetics (whether within the environment or within landscape images) – involves atavistic responses to environmental stimuli. Jay Appleton's *The Experience of Landscape* (John Wiley: London, 1975) sees aesthetic responses to landscape as atavistic survivals from the days when life itself depended upon the recognition of safe terrain. Certainly, the subjective impact of landscape is closely related to the study of environmental perception. Whether or not artists do have heightened levels of awareness of their surroundings is debatable, but many writers certainly have a highly developed sense of place. Landscape has often been depicted as an essential ingredient in an evocation of surroundings, so novels may well be a useful source for landscape images: for example, Zane Grey's western, *Riders of the Purple Sage* (1912) (Penguin: Harmondsworth, 1990), and Robie Macauley's post-Holocaust midwestern novel, *The Secret History of Time to Come* (Corgi: London, 1983). For an introduction to the way in which settlers responded to the interplay between their expectations, the harsh physical surroundings and an often merciless economic system – and, in so doing, created a distinctive regional landscape – Walter Prescott Webb, *The Great Plains* (Ginn: New York, 1931), remains a classic, and is itself explored by G. M. Tobin, 'Landscape, Region, and the Writing of History: Walter Prescott Webb in the 1920s', *American Studies International* 4/XVI (Summer 1978), pp. 7–18. How did people respond to the opening up of the prairies and their eventual decay into a dust bowl? The remarkable scale of so much of the prairies suggests to many writers that nature is an actor, not a backdrop, a theme very similar to that of the historian Frederick Jackson Turner (see W. van T. Clark, 'The Western Novel: A Symposium', ed. J. R. Milton, *South Dakota Review* 2 (Autumn 1964)). Local writers have sought to detail the impact of the western vastness upon lives grappling with such an array of novel surroundings (people, places and things). The landscape is seen as a force to be reckoned with, enjoying almost a character of its own. Space is no mere setting, no mere backdrop, but an overpowering presence – the vastness of the plains, the height of the peaks, the distance of the horizons. What is being evoked is a presence, like an ancient deity active in people's lives, without whose intervention nothing that is said or done makes any sense.

One such writer was Willa Cather, who, in books such as *My Antonia* (1918) and *Death Comes for the Archbishop* (1927), describes the desolation of the plains, where nature was a form of incompleteness, of wilderness. In such harsh surroundings, everything had to be created. When circumstances worsened into ecological and social collapse, this seemed like some kind of divine malevolence, punishment for who knows what. Landscape was an essentially human creation: land tamed out of wilderness. John Steinbeck also portrayed the prairies and their ecological collapse in *Grapes of Wrath* (1939), followed the next year by John Ford's film version, which brought a certain set of images to the public, images originally from government research projects which have now become part of the way in which Americans view the 1930s. The ecological history of this tragedy is carefully explored in Donald Worster, *Dust Bowl: The Southern Plains in the 1930s* (Oxford University Press: New York, 1979), which contains many of the classic photographs of the area. For an evocative musical record, try Woody Guthrie's *Dust Bowl Ballads* (1940; recently reissued by Folkways), many of which were re-recorded by Bob Dylan in the 1960s, Ry Cooder in the 1970s, and Nanci Griffith in the 1990s, and have had considerable influence upon the themes explored by Bruce Springsteen in his *Nebraska* and *the ghost of tom joad* recordings.

A growing literature explores the role of landscape imagery in the frontier experience. One such example is David A. Lanegran, 'The Pioneer's View of the Frontier as Presented in the Regional Novel *Giants in the Earth*', in *International Geography* (University of Toronto Press: Toronto, 1972), pp. 350–2. For a general overview, see Fred Langman, 'Landscape and Identity in the American Novel', *American Studies International* 4/XVI (Summer 1978), pp. 34–47. Classics that are usually remembered for other motifs are increasingly being examined in terms of their landscape elements. James Fenimore Cooper's *The Pioneers* (1823), *The Last of the Mohicans* (1826), *The Prairie* (1827), and *The Deerslayer* (1841) are deeply engaged with a sense that the frontier, its peoples and its landscapes, are about to undergo unprecedented change. For a general overview, see L. Lockwood Hazard and F. Ungar, *The*

Frontier in American Literature (New York Press: New York, 1967), and Christopher L. Salter and William J. Lloyd, *Landscape in Literature* (Association of American Geographers: Washington DC, 1976). For a specific exploration, see Blake Nevius, *Cooper's Landscapes* (University of California Press, Berkeley, 1976). A more sophisticated series of essays show how far landscape studies have moved in a very few years: Mick Gidley and Robert Lawson-Peebles (eds), *Views of American Landscapes* (Cambridge University Press: Cambridge, 1989). For travellers' images of the frontier, see J. A. Jackle, *Images of the Ohio Valley: An Historical Geography of Travel, 1740–1860* (Oxford University Press: New York, 1977), followed by his subsequent study *The Tourist: Travel in Twentieth-Century North America* (University of Nebraska Press: Lincoln, 1985). For a British view, see Christopher Mulvey, *Anglo-American Landscapes* (Cambridge University Press: Cambridge, 1983).

Many anthropologists and archaeologists study the modern landscape with great care as they seek to re-create, in their own minds, on paper and, increasingly, in open-air museums, earlier environments. There is a considerable and growing debate over the way in which artefacts recovered from within the landscape can usefully be interpreted to reconstruct the past. Christopher Tilley (ed.), *Reading Material Culture* (Basil Blackwell: Oxford, 1990), explores the way in which Barthes, Lévi-Strauss, and Foucault treat the interpretation of material, of which the landscape can be considered a composite. Daniel Miller, *Material Culture and Mass Consumption* (Basil Blackwell: Oxford, 1991), argues that people redefine the elements of the world around them to make it express both themselves and their cultures. Both texts illustrate the similarity of approaches by archaeologists and landscape analysts, teasing out the complex relationships between material objects and social practices. Such approaches to landscapes are increasingly part of an interest in 'history from the bottom up', an interest in those Americans who did not become famous, create great monuments, or leave lengthy written expositions of their thoughts and values. Artefacts are often the only surviving record of the vast majority of people. Thus, many social historians seeking a usable past have sought to investigate the landscape as a collection of such artefacts. In this, they have found a common cause with architectural historians, anthropologists, folklorists, historical preservationists and geographers. A concern for the vernacular is a concern for all facets and types of landscapes, from Williamsburg's 'living history' museum to Los Angeles's shopping malls and hamburger stands.

Until fairly recently, however, studies of vernacular architecture have tended to be strongly antiquarian, with little or no attempt to place vernacular buildings in their historical – never mind their landscape – contexts. Architectural survivals tended to be discussed in high-art terms, and to be titled *The Old Houses of My State*. The least unsatisfactory of these older surveys is T. T. Waterman's *The Dwellings of Colonial America* (University of North Carolina Press: Chapel Hill, 1950). In place of any historical context, such antiquarian accounts substituted an interest in materials and building technologies – the use of timber frames and brick types, for instance. An interesting modern example of this can be found in Dell Upton's 'Traditional Timber Framing: An Interpretative Essay', in Brooke Hindle (ed.), *The Material Culture of the Wooden Age* (Sleepy Hollow Press: Tarrytown, New York, 1981).

Geographers have been among those who have expanded this interest in buildings to explore cultural history. A classic is Henry Glassie's *Patterns in the Material Folk Culture of the Eastern United States* (University of Pennsylvania Press: Philadelphia, 1969). This spatial concern has its flowering in the work of Fred Kniffen, who was particularly interested in the way in which folk housing types diffused across the country in frontier days. The classic study is his 'Folk Housing: Key to Diffusion', *Annals of the Association of American Geographers* 55 (1965), pp. 549–77. Unfortunately for landscape students, this concern for the process of technological diffusion, whilst placing vernacular structures within an analytic framework, tended to leave landscape issues *per se* to one side, as if the landscape were merely the sum of all its parts. The literature became full of studies of covered bridges, barns, and quoins (ways of interweaving intersecting walls). Sometimes these features are indeed regionally distinctive, but they are used more to delineate a regional impact of a distinct group than to explore the totality of the landscape within which these features occur, as in Richard V. Francaviglia's 'Mormon Central-Hall Houses in the American West', *Annals of the Association of American Geographers* 61 (1971), pp. 65–71, or Roger Welsch's *Sodwalls: The Story of the Nebraska Sod House* (Purchells: Broken Bow, Nebraska, 1968). A classic in this genre is Terry Jordan's *Texas Log Buildings: A Folk Architecture* (University of Texas Press: Austin, 1978).

Folklorists and social historians have grappled with the way in which innovations are introduced into a traditional repertoire. How did Renaissance ideas of symmetry and design influence folk (rather than public or upper-class) buildings? Henry Glassie explored this in 'Eighteenth-Century Cultural Processes in Delaware Valley Folk Building' in *Winterthur* 7 (1972). How material culture helped to reproduce or transform cultural forms is only just beginning to be explored. Ian M. G. Quimby's edited collection of essays starts this off: *Material Culture and the Study of American Life* (Norton: New York, 1978). The most obvious links between landscape artefacts and ideology may be seen in studies of Utopian communities, such as Dolores Hayden, *Seven American Utopias: The Architecture of Communitarian Socialism, 1790–1975* (MIT Press: Cambridge, Mass., 1976). For that most famous of communities, the Mormons, start with James L. Wescoat, Jr., 'Challenging the Desert', and James E. Vance, Jr., 'Democratic Utopia and the American Landscape', both in Conzen (ed.), *The Making of the American Landscape*, pp. 186–203, 204–20. For debate on the interpretation of the Mormon cultural impact, see D. W. Meinig, 'The Mormon Culture Region: Strategies and Patterns in the Geography of the American West, 1847–1964', *Annals of the Association of American Geographers* 55 (1965), pp. 191–220. For a single volume, see R. V. Francaviglia, *The Mormon Landscape: Existence, Creation, and Perception of a Unique Image of the American West* (AMS: New York, 1978). An important, though undervalued, analytical piece uses the example of the Dutch fundamentalists of western Michigan to explore the way in which ideologies are turned into landscapes and the way in which landscapes can be read for their ideological imprint: E. M. Bjorklund, 'Ideology and Culture', *Annals of the Association of American Geographers* 54 (June 1964), pp. 227–41.

Much concern for architectural form has tended to stress survivalism: particular buildings may not survive much longer, but they should at least be recorded. A typical result would be Constance M. Greiff, *Lost America* (Pyne Press: Princeton, 1974). With the increased interest in ethnic roots, such studies are ever more popular, whether Jordan's analysis of German forms in Texas, or John M. Vlach, 'The Shotgun House: An African Architectural Legacy', in D. Upton and J. M. Vlach (eds), *Common Places: Readings in American Vernacular Architecture* (University of Georgia Press: Athens, 1986), pp. 58–78. Most studies of particular architectural forms have, until recently, tended to 'assume that buildings are the concrete products of mental attempts to conceptualize and solve architectural problems', according to Dell Upton, 'Ordinary Buildings: A Bibliographical Essay in American Vernacular

Architecture', *American Studies International* 19/2 (Winter 1981), pp. 57–75. Designs were assumed to be functional – new ideas are accepted 'to make a better mousetrap'. For a rebuttal of functionalist determinism and a recognition that all objects incorporate aesthetic decisions which, to some degree, reflect the cultural values that shape both functional and decorative elements, see Amos Rapoport's *House Form and Culture* (Prentice-Hall: Englewood Cliffs, NJ, 1969).

Though historians have been able to identify common architectural types from a vast variety of buildings, how are such types related both to the natural topography and to each other within the landscape? If buildings and their layout express the culture that created them, then landscapes (as language) may have identifiable rules of syntax, internal structures and meanings. This assumption has seeped into architectural and landscape studies from archaeology, linguistics and the study of popular culture. The way in which people and buildings relate to one another has also been explored by Edward Hall in *The Hidden Dimension* (Anchor Books: New York, 1969), where the spaces between people and buildings are seen as significant clues through which people express their feelings about each other. An interest in the way in which people interact with their surroundings is not as recent as many might believe. Walter Firey ('Sentiment and Symbolism as Ecological Variables', *American Sociological Review* 10 (1945), pp. 140–8) recognised that human attachment to place acts as a major factor in influencing landscape change. Similarly, Kevin Lynch explored the way in which people distinguish urban neighbourhoods through the layout of streets, building styles, and boundary markers in *Images of the City* (MIT Press: Cambridge, Mass., 1960).

A recent trend has been to expand the term 'vernacular' to include any building that was not built in a self-conscious attempt to express a particular architectural tradition or set of principles. However, a concern for the survival of traditional buildings and historical landscapes has tended to divert attention away from the modern vernacular, reflecting an élite preoccupation with the aesthetically uplifting view. Conferences on Appalachian culture ignore the proliferation of satellite dishes in favour of more acceptable traditional features, such as bridges (preferably covered). Fortunately, this tradition of treating landscapes as morally uplifting illustrations for the benefit of outsiders has not gone unchallenged. Landscape students are increasingly interested in reading the whole text, satellite dishes and all. Such down-to-earth concerns have been encouraged in the USA by J. B. Jackson. His journal *Landscape* reflects a growing interest in the meanings of Americans' everyday surroundings, encouraging an interest in everyday objects within ordinary, rather than spectacular, landscapes. Probably the best overview is his own *Discovering the Vernacular Landscape* (Yale University Press: New Haven, 1984). For a discussion of pre-industrial vernacular landscapes, see John R. Stilgoe, *Common Landscape of America, 1580–1845* (Yale University Press: New Haven, 1982). Backyards, gas stations, motels, fast-food outlets: all emerge as interesting to the degree that they are anchored in daily life. Here, then, is no concern for outsiders' aesthetic responses, but a desire to explore the landscape as a place for living and working. J. Belaso has unashamedly explored the modern commercial landscape in *Americans on the Road – From Autocamp to Motel, 1910–1945* (MIT Press: Cambridge, Mass., 1979), of particular interest to Bates Motel aficionados. For a similar exploration, see D. I. Vieyra's *Fill 'Er Up: An Architectural History of America's Gas Stations* (Macmillan: New York, 1979), or Richard Pillsbury, *From Boarding House to Bistro: The American Restaurant Then and Now* (Unwin Hyman: London, 1990). The modern 'strip', that long avenue of car showrooms, fast-food outlets and motels at the edge of every town, is explored in R. Venturi, *Vegas: The Forgotten Symbolism of Architectural Form* (MIT Press: Cambridge, Mass., 1977), though the city itself should perhaps be approached by way of Tom Wolfe, *The Kandy-Colored Tangerine-Flake Streamline Baby* (Farrar Straus and Giroux: New York, 1965), before venturing into the spate of mid-1990s Vegas movies, of which *Honey, I Blew Up the Kids* is far from the most vacuous.

How typical or symbolic of wider US values are such supposedly all-American icons? Many commentators abhor and, therefore, ignore them; others claim that, for good or ill, they are quintessentially American: to read the syntax of their creation is to gain access to the deep logic of America's psyche. Others have been fascinated with the cross-country journey, Kerouac-style. Try Thomas and Geraldine Vale, *Western Images: Western Landscapes: Travels along US 89* (University of Arizona Press: Tuscon, 1990). However, an over-simplistic fascination for the 'Americanness' of any one particular landscape can surely be left to the British Sunday colour supplements, with their desire to promote a 'funny foreigners doing weird things' view of America. A more useful approach to ordinary American surroundings can be found in K. T. Jackson's study of suburbia, called, with just a touch of irony,

The Crabgrass Frontier (Oxford University Press: New York, 1985). Further aspects of the modern vernacular can be seen in M. Fishwick and J. M. Neil, *Popular Architecture* (Popular Press: Bowling Green, Ohio, 1976). For a useful compilation of J. B. Jackson's attempts to explore the everyday rather than merely icons, see Ervin H. Zube (ed.), *Landscapes: Selected Writings of J. B. Jackson* (University of Massachusetts Press: Amhurst, 1970).

Ordinary surroundings can seem extraordinarily exotic – even threatening – to those outside American society. How did immigrants make sense of the Anglo-American landscape forms within which they came to live, and to what extent did they succeed in reinterpreting and re-forming their surroundings? Some work has been done on immigrant responses to public open spaces, as in Roy Rosenzweig's *Eight Hours for What We Will: Workers and Leisure in an Industrial City, 1870–1920* (Harvard University Press: Cambridge, Mass., 1983). How did the availability of new industrial technologies influence existing vernacular architecture? Did pattern books and mail-order houses really eradicate Anglo-American folk architecture, as is so often suggested? Surely the interchange was more subtle and complex? The survival of Hispanic styles in the south-west would suggest that Anglo-styles could also have survived, beyond being merely relict features, given a sufficiently high group attachment to their continued presence.

Another field worthy of consideration concerns the interrelations between the geography of exterior landscape and interior spaces, particularly the home, the office and the factory. There has been a start with David E. Sopher, 'The Landscape of Home: Myth, Experience, Social Meaning', in Meinig (ed.), *Interpreting Ordinary Landscapes*, along with Douglas Porteous, 'Home: The Territorial Core', *Geographical Review* 66/4 (October 1976), pp. 383–90. See also D. Geoffrey Haywood, 'Home as an Environmental and Psychological Concept', *Landscape* 20/1 (October 1975), pp. 2–9. An interesting connection with Victorian culture can be seen in G. Wright, *Moralism and the Model Home: Domestic Architecture and Cultural Conflict in Chicago, 1873–1913* (University of Chicago Press: Chicago, 1980). For a mid-western case study, see Joseph S. Wood, 'Cultural Meaning in a Common House', *North American Culture* II/2 (1986), pp. 77–86. Many of the philosophical ideas involved are explored by Yi-Fu Tuan, as in 'Place: An Experiential Perspective', *Geographical Review* 65/2 (April 1975), pp. 151–65.

There is no single volume that deals adequately with the US landscape in all its variety and the many forms through which it has been represented. There are many regional geography textbooks that deal with the landscape in passing, but most of these are not explicitly concerned to explore landscape creation, variation and interpretation *per se*. Even Stephen S. Birdsall and John W. Florin, *Regional Landscapes of the United States and Canada* (John Wiley: New York, 1992) is more of an old-style regional text than a landscape exploration. For a British readership, the most readable and readily available remains John Paterson, *North America*, 4th edn (Oxford University Press: Oxford, 1989). The chapters on Appalachia and the Southwest are probably the most explicitly concerned with landscape; elsewhere, the concern is more often with demographic change and urbanisation. The cover, showing the famous mid-western grid pattern, is probably worth the price of the book alone. Many other texts have sought to challenge Paterson's market leadership, both here and in the USA. Most do so by being concerned with 'relevance', exploring topics such as poverty and development at the expense of overt consideration of regional landscape variation. Of these, Michael Bradshaw, *Regions and Regionalism in America* (Macmillan: London, 1988), is the most readily available, reasonably priced, while addressing a UK audience. Less concerned to be immediately relevant, Wilbur Zelinsky, *The Cultural Geography of the United States*, 2nd edn (Prentice Hall: Englewood Cliffs, NJ, 1992), is stimulating and deeply concerned to explore the cultural landscape in terms of its expression of US values and conflicts, though, like so many other human geography texts, it is never fully focused on the landscape as such, being more interested in identifying patterns within the landscape. However, for outlining US values and characteristics that are evident within the landscape, it remains worth reading.

For an explicit exploration of the landscape idea, with some provocative discussion of American landscapes, see Denis Cosgrove, *Social Formation and Symbolic Landscape* (Croom Helm: London, 1984). The title is almost the most formidable part of the book, which explores both what we mean by landscape and how this way of ordering experience has emerged from a long history of representation. The case studies of Renaissance Italy and England inform his exploration of US landscape traditions. The final chapters on 'Sublime Nature: Landscape and Industrial Capitalism' and 'The Landscape Idea in the Modern World' are excellent, and can be brought directly to bear upon the US experience. The bibliography is wonderfully comprehensive and would make a useful purchasing yardstick for any library wishing to support landscape studies.

For those wishing to focus entirely upon the creation of the USA as a place, the most accessible text is Conzen (ed.), *The Making of the American Landscape*, a series of essays, plus an excellent and extensive bibliography, written by a wide range of US landscape enthusiasts. There is really no rival collection, though its failure to deal with images of the landscape is inexcusable, especially given the use of a landscape painting on the cover, illustrating the still too prevalent habit of seeing images as little more than filler illustrations.

For those interested in going beyond Stanley W. Trimble's 'Nature's Continent', in Conzen (ed.), *The Making of the American Landscape*, pp. 27–50, try the books from various television series: Ron Redfern, *The Making of a Continent* (BBC: London, 1983), or Robert Peck, *Land of the Eagle* (BBC: London, 1990). The latter is particularly recommended for approaching natural history through an account of the human occupation of various ecological niches. Both books are greatly enhanced if used alongside the video versions. A more traditional, but suitably concise, physical overview can be found in Paterson, *North America*. An excellent essay on the Indian legacy is available in Conzen (ed.), *The Making of the American Landscape*, with a regional case study in William Cronon, *Changes in the Land: Indians, Colonists and the Ecology of New England* (Hill and Wang: New York, 1983). For an excellent multifaceted slice through the US landscape, see Michael Williams, *Americans and their Forests* (Cambridge University Press: Cambridge, 1989). For a classic study of modern ecological collapse, see Donald Worster's *Dust Bowl* (Oxford University Press: New York, 1979).

The origins of New England's distinctiveness are introduced in Douglas R. McManis, *Colonial New England* (Oxford University Press: New York, 1975), with a brilliant exploration of the changing imagery of its landscapes presented by Joseph S. Wood, ' "Build, Therefore, Your Own World": The New England Village as Settlement Ideal', *Annals of the Association of American Geographers* 81/1 (1991), pp. 32–50. Joel Garreau has a stimulating contemporary essay in his *Nine Nations of North America* (Avon: New York, 1989). Useful introductions to the contrasting landscapes of north and south are offered by Peirce Lewis and Sam Hilliard in Conzen (ed.), *The Making of the American Landscape*. See also Hilliard's 'Plantations Created the South', *Geographical*

Magazine 52 (1980), pp. 409–16. Hildegaard Johnson pulls together some varied contributions to explore the creation of a new national landscape in the old Northwest Territory, now the Midwest, *Order upon the Land: the US Rectangular Land Survey and the Upper Mississippi* (Oxford University Press: New York, 1976). Much the same ground is covered in Sam B. Hilliard's 'A Robust New Nation, 1783–1820', in Robert D. Mitchell and Paul A. Groves (eds), *North America: The Changing Geography of a Changing Continent* (Hutchinson: London, 1987), pp. 149–71). Robert Lawson-Peebles confirms that American revolutionary culture, as seen in both imaginative literature and non-literary writings, sought to impose a Utopian design suitable for a new republic and, in so doing, created a peculiarly American landscape even where such ambitions were thwarted. Modern cultural implications are explored brilliantly in J. B. Jackson, 'The Order of a Landscape: Reason and Religion in Newtonian America', in Meinig (ed.), *Interpreting Ordinary Landscapes*, pp. 153–63. The extent to which American culture reflects British origins and American surroundings is a long-standing debate. A novel twist has been introduced by Terry G. Jordan and Matti Kaups, with their belief that the most crucial cultural element along the frontier was actually a Scandinavian log cabin: *The American Backwoods Frontier: An Ethnic and Ecological Interpretation* (The Johns Hopkins Press: Baltimore, 1989). Sceptics should visit the open-air Danish folk museum just outside Copenhagen.

While Anglo- and African Americans were creating an America on the east coast, other imperial legacies were being established to the west. Though there is no study of Russian America that deals specifically with landscape impact, such topics are dealt with in passing throughout James R. Gibson, *Imperial Russia in Frontier America: The Changing Geography of Supply of Russian America, 1784–1867* (Oxford University Press: New York, 1976). For the Spanish legacy, start with David Hornbeck, 'Spanish Legacy in the Borderlands', in Conzen (ed.), *The Making of the American Landscape*, pp. 51–62. Alvar W. Carlson, *The Spanish-American Homeland: Four Centuries in New Mexico's Rio Arriba* (The Johns Hopkins University Press: Baltimore, 1990), deals with the impact and survival of those Spanish peoples trapped within the USA by the treaty of 1848. For excellent regional case studies, see D. W. Meinig's *Imperial Texas* (University of Texas Press: Austin, 1969), and *The Southwest: Three Peoples in Geographical Change, 1600–1970* (Oxford University Press: New York, 1971), though landscape is never quite the central focus of these studies. A useful discussion of the landscape impact of French life in the New World can be found in R. C. Harris and J. Warkeutin, *Canada before Confederation* (Oxford University Press: New York, 1974). Cole Harris, 'French Landscapes in North America', in Conzen (ed.), *The Making of the American Landscape*, pp. 63–79, is an excellent and well-focused introduction to this topic.

More philosophical considerations of landscapes can usefully be considered, starting with Peirce Lewis, 'Axioms for Reading the Landscape', in Meinig (ed.), *Interpreting Ordinary Landscapes*, where the appropriateness of literary-based metaphors, using such terms as 'texts', 'authors', 'motifs', and even 'sub-texts', is raised. Specifically American aspects of reading the landscape can be followed through David Lowenthal, 'The American Scene', *Geographical Review* 58 (1968), pp. 61–88, a thoughtful essay on why the USA looks the way it does and what the landscape may be able to tell us about American culture. For a focus on rural American, try J. Fraser Hart, *The Look of the Land* (Prentice-Hall: Englewood Cliffs, NJ, 1974).

The most widely known landscape text remains Hoskins, *The Making of the English Landscape*, a book which still influences the exploration of landscapes far beyond Hoskins's almost parochial concerns: witness the echo of his title in Conzen's American text. In discussing the societies that formed the landscape, Hoskins created an intellectual legacy that is recognised in D. W. Meinig, 'Reading the Landscape: An Appreciation of W. G. Hoskins and J. B. Jackson', in Meinig (ed.), *Interpreting Ordinary Landscapes*, and by Marwyn S. Samuels in his essay, 'The Biography of Landscape', in the same collection. Hoskins's original text has been updated, via a series of annotations by Christopher Taylor, in the 1988 hardback edition, an innovative way of demonstrating how perceived ideas can change, often quite radically, with further research, while retaining the flavour of the quirky original.

Many consider the attraction of landscape analysis to lie in the 'view of the past' that it supposedly offers to the skilled observer. David Lowenthal is a crucial interpreter of past landscapes, both in the UK (his academic base) and in his native USA. His recent classic is *The Past is a Foreign Country* (Cambridge University Press: Cambridge, 1985), which develops ideas that were raised in his essay, 'Past Time, Present Place: Landscape and Memory', *Geographical Review* 65 (1975), pp. 1–36. The use of the term 'symbolic landscapes' is a recognition that certain landscapes seem to have a power over and beyond their roles within the physical and ecological systems of which they are a part. That is, they come to have a power upon the mind and imagination of people who have never even visited the place itself. The classic study is Elizabeth McKinsey, *Niagara Falls: Icon of the Sublime* (Cambridge University Press: Cambridge, 1985), the modern-resort aspects of which are followed up by Rob Shields, *Places on the Margin: Alternative Geographies of Modernity* (Routledge: London, 1991). Alan Trachtenberg's *Brooklyn Bridge: Fact and Symbol* (University of Chicago Press: Chicago, 1979), and *The Statue of Liberty* (Allen Lane: London, 1976), explore specific New York icons, while John A. Jackle looks at the whole skyline's iconic status in 'The Metropolis as an Attraction', in *The Tourist: Travel in Twentieth-Century North America* (University of Nebraska Press: Lincoln, 1985), pp. 263–85. For an overview-cum-discussion of the relationship between landscape and iconography, see the introduction in Stephen Daniels and Denis Cosgrove (eds), *The Iconography of Landscape* (Cambridge University Press: Cambridge, 1988). For an interesting exploration of these ideas as they have come to focus upon the western lands, see Max Oelschlaeger, *The Idea of Wilderness: From Prehistory to the Age of Ecology* (Yale University Press: New Haven, 1991). For concern about the impact of ever more powerful technologies on ever more fragile western ecosystems, see the essays by Williams, Hudson and Westcoast in Conzen (ed.), *The Making of the American Landscape*. The way in which painting was involved in a debate about the natural world is explored in Barbara Novak, *Nature and Culture: American Landscape and Painting, 1825–1875* (Thames and Hudson: London, 1980).

The wilderness remains a deeply cherished American theme, a challenge to Europe's cultural treasures. Though the classic exploration of these ideas remains Henry Nash Smith, *Virgin Land: The American West as Symbol and Myth* (Harvard University Press: Cambridge, Mass., 1950), there has been a great deal of subsequent work that is worth investigating. Effective overviews can be found within Alfred Runte, 'The West: Wealth, Wonderland and Wilderness', in J. Wreford Watson and T. O'Riordan (eds), *The American Environment: Perceptions and Policies* (John Wiley: London, 1976), pp. 47–62, and L. H. Graber, *Wilderness as Sacred Space* (Association of American Geographers Monograph Series, No. 8: Washington DC, 1976). More developed theses are presented in R. Nash, *Wilderness and the American Mind* (Yale University Press: New Haven, 1973), and Oelschlaeger, *The Idea of Wilderness*.

The landscape photograph is explored in John Szarkowski (ed.), *The Photographer and the American Landscape* (Museum of Modern Art: New York, 1963), E. Jussin and E. Lindquist-Cook, *Landscape as Photography* (Yale University Press: New Haven, 1985). An interesting influence is explored in Elizabeth Lindquist-Cook, *The Influence of Photography on American Landscape Painting, 1839–1880* (Garland: New York, 1972). For photography in and of the West, see Weston J. Naef and James N. Wood, *Era of Exploitation: The Rise of Landscape Photography in the West, 1860–85* (New York Graphic Society: Boston, 1975), Karen Current and William Current, *Photographs and the Old West* (Henry Abrams: New York, 1978), and Ralph W. Andres, *Photographers of the Frontier West* (Bonanza: New York, 1965). For the 1930s, see Roy Emerson Stryker and Nancy Wood, *In this Proud Land: America, 1935–1943 as Seen in the FSA Photographs* (New York Graphic Society: Greenwich, Conn., 1973). For studies of, arguably, the most popular landscape photographer, see Lilane de Cock (ed.), *Ansel Adams* (Morgan and Morgan: Hastings, NY, 1972), or Nancy Newhall, *Ansel Adams: The Eloquent Light* (The Sierra Club: San Francisco, 1963).

There is no substitute for actually seeing the American landscape. Bizarre copies can sometimes be found in Europe, such as Disneyland Paris, drive-in McDonalds, or the rodeo area at the American Adventure theme park near Derby. Other copies are promoted for educational rather than entertainment uses, such as the colonial garden at Bath's American Museum, or the frontier settlement at Omagh's Ulster American Folk Park. All are worth experiencing with an informed and sceptical eye. For American paintings and photographic images in UK galleries, there is no single catalogue source. US painters and photographers turn up within gallery displays, but in no systematic fashion. More accessible, for research at least, are the US collections increasingly available in micro-form. The FSA prints are available on microfilm, all 250,000 of them! The 54,000 prints from the New York Public Library are available from University Microfilms International. In the UK, high school and college teachers may borrow slides from the American Studies Resource Centres at the Liverpool Community College (Riverside Campus), soon to be part of the Liverpool John Moores University. For other suggestions, see Mick Gidley, *American Photography* (British Association for American Studies Pamphlet No. 12, 1983).

I have already attempted to summarise a vast literature on US cities in 'Profile of the American City', in Dennis Welland (ed.), *The United*

States: A Companion to American Studies (Methuen: London, 1987), pp. 54–86. Though many writers deal with those processes that help to create, shape and redefine the urban landscape, few deal with the landscape so overtly or so intelligently as Edward Relph, *The Modern Urban Landscape* (Croom Helm: Beckenham, 1987). Even David Schuyler's *The New Urban Landscape* (The Johns Hopkins University Press: Baltimore, 1986) is more accurately described by its subtitle, 'The Redefinition of City Form in Nineteenth-Century America', a far more constrained enterprise. For many years the most accessible text to deal with the urban landscape in detail, albeit still implicitly, was Sam Bass Warner, *The Urban Wilderness* (Harper: New York, 1972), contrasting the development of New York City, Chicago, and Los Angeles through a vast array of photographic material. Irving Culter, *Chicago: Metropolis of the Mid-Continent* (Kendall-Hunt: Dubuque, Iowa, 1976) also presents a wide array of photographic details, though again it does not deal explicitly with landscape. Large cities are well featured in the various volumes of J. S. Adams (ed.), *Contemporary Metropolitan America: Twenty Geographical Vignettes* (Ballinger: Cambridge, Mass., 1976). Many are published separately in paperback. They are a mixed bag: Peirce Lewis's on New Orleans is warmly recommended. There is a vast literature on the Sunbelt, such as David C. Perry and Alfred J. Watkins, *The Rise of the Sunbelt Cities* (Sage: Beverly Hills, 1977), but there is little overt concern for specifically landscape development; rather, this has to be inferred from changes in transportation systems, economic activity, and population distribution.

This growing shift in US life is placed within a wider context in David Clark, *Post-Industrial America: A Geographical Perspective* (Methuen: London, 1985), though landscape issues remain, paradoxically, both central to his case and rarely of explicit concern, demonstrating how landscape is still widely regarded as unproblematic, a self-evident and obvious text to be read for what it suggests about more complex issues. Many people who write about the urban environment are, of course, not interested in landscape studies *per se*. Nevertheless, they often provide excellent analyses of the way in which massive landscape change has come to take place: for instance, Kenneth Fox, *Metropolitan America: Urban Life and Urban Policy in the United States, 1940–1980* (Macmillan: Basingstoke, 1985), which deals with suburban expansion, inner-city decay, and urban redevelopment in ways that link the concerns of political scientists, geographers, and all those

interested in urban landscapes. Ways in which specific, large-scale projects have been put together are dealt with in Michael N. Danielson and
James W. Doig, *New York: The Politics of Urban Regional Development*
(University of California Press: Berkeley, 1982). For a case study from
the Reagan years, see Paul L. Knox, 'The Restless Urban Landscape:
Economic and Socio-Cultural Change and the Transformation of Metropolitan Washington DC', *Annals of the Association of the American
Geographers* 81/2 (June 1991), pp. 181–209. For readers who have
already been stimulated by the Baltimore-based work of David Harveys,
Conditions of Postmodernity (Blackwell: London, 1989), a treat awaits:
the growing urban-based analyses focused upon the Los Angeles experience. For an introduction, try J. E. Vance, 'California and the Search
for the Ideal', *Annals of the Association of American Geographers* 62 (1972),
pp. 185–210, before moving on to Reyner Banham, *Los Angeles: The
Architecture of Four Ecologies* (Penguin: Harmondsworth, 1971). The
most exciting works have to be Mike Davis, *City of Quartz: Excavating
the Future of Los Angeles* (Verso: London, 1990), and Edward Soja,
Postmodern Geographies (Verso: New York, 1989). For those readers
who like their dystopic spaces to be up-market, one of the most accessible
discussions of shopping malls, theme parks and other quasi-public spaces
can be found in the highly readable Michael Sorkin (ed.), *Variations on
a Theme Park: A New American City and the End of Public Space* (Noonday: New York, 1992). Those wishing to place such new types of places
and spaces in a more theoretical context, try Pamela Shurmer-Smith
and Kevin Hannam, *Worlds of Desire, Realms of Power: A Cultural
Geography* (Edward Arnold: London, 1994). This book should be quite
a surprise to those who still expect to find cultural geography as little
more than a cataloguing of exotic ethnicity, with its discussion of com-
modified spaces and monuments. All discussion of post-modern
landscapes, however, makes interesting comparison with Ridley Scott's
1993 reissue of his Los Angeles-based dystopic film, *Bladerunner*, or
even with the various space stations in the *Aliens* movie trilogy.

The above suggestions cannot hope to do justice to a field that has
expanded almost out of recognition since the late 1980s amd continues
to do so in the early 1990s. The landscapes of popular culture alone are
worth at least a further volume. There are the replica landscapes that
have actually been created, such as world fairs, fun fairs and theme parks
on the one hand, and open-air museums on the other; there are also the
imaginary landscapes created by the mass media, such as the frontier

lands of the western or the cityscape of gangsters and cops; and, as with
all landscape studies, there is the interaction between these two facets,
the landscape of the imagination and its impact on the landscape of the
built environment. A useful introduction to the role of world fairs from
a mainly European standpoint can be obtained in Paul Greenhalgh,
*Ephemeral Vistas: The Expositions Universelles, Great Exhibitions and
World Fairs, 1851–1939* (Manchester University Press: Manchester,
1988). For a perspective from North America, see Robert W. Rydell,
All the World's a Fair (University of Chicago Press: Chicago, 1984),
and his excellent follow-up, *World of Fairs: The Century-of-Progress
Expositions* (University of Chicago Press: Chicago, 1993). Private developers have also sought to capitalise upon the growing mass market
for outdoor sites. Coney Island on New York's Atlantic seashore was
both a reaction against up-market themes at world fairs and the creation
of a reaction against such down-market sites, a major factor in the
emergence of the modern theme park. For Coney Island, see John
F. Kasson, *Amusing the Million* (Hill and Wang: New York, 1978). For
theme parks, try Richard Francaviglia, 'Main Street USA: A Compari-
son/Contrast in Streetscapes in Disneyland and Walt Disney World',
Journal of Popular Culture 15 (1981), pp. 141–56. For an initial attempt
to see theme parks within a complex pedigree of world fairs and theme
parks, see Stephen F. Mills, 'Disney and the Promotions of Synthetic
Worlds', *American Studies International* 28/2 (October 1990), pp. 66–79.
For just a sample of the voluminous literature on the western, try Kim
Newman, *Wild West Movies: How the West was Found, Won, Lost, Lied
about, Filmed and Forgotten* (Bloomsbury: London, 1990). Better still,
visit the American Museum in Bath, for a serious, high-culture view of
the American experience, which includes the re-creation of an American
garden, and then visit Derbyshire's theme park 'The American Adventure', to see the way in which landscape themes are reworked within
mass culture. The best, of course, is to experience the variety of US
landscapes first-hand, travelling around the country itself. If all else fails,
visit the National Museum of Photography, Film and Television in
Bradford, or the Smithsonian Museum in Washington DC for their
spectacular 70 mm IMAX movies such as 'The Wonder of Flight',
'Niagara' or 'The Grand Canyon'.

Notes

1. This still widespread habit of using the term 'landscape as a as catch-all, but eye-catching, phrase continues with Tony Bodger, Walter Edgar and Jan Nordby Gretlund (eds), *Southern Landscape* (Stauffenburg Verlag: Tobingen, 1996), a recent volume that seems initially to be focused upon southern landscapes. On investigation, however, 'landscape' turns out to be such a catch-all phrase that it is useless. Only one essay seems to have any awareness of the field of landscape studies, though some do focus upon specific elements within the landscape. The title seems to resemble those book covers that promise everything, but deliver something else.
2. UNESCO has traditionally used 'landscape' in terms of the environmental impact of human activity, as in *The Man-Made Landscape* (UNESCO: Paris, 1977). Stonehenge or Abu Simbel, landmarks to be saved from destruction by limiting access to them or by removal to a place of safety, are typical of such concerns.
3. See Hubert B. Owen, 'Regional Planning – An Example from the United States, *ibid.*, pp. 127–53.

Index

Adams, Ansel, 61, 138
Alaska, 23, 25, 53
America as Arcadia, 16–17, 57
American Dream, 1
American Studies, 5, 7
Amish, 9, 27, 43n
Appalachia, 3–4, 13, 14, 22
Appleton, Jay, 70n

Baltimore redevelopment, 83
battlefields, 9, 107–8
Brooklyn Bridge, 71, 84–6, 137
Bryant, William Cullen, 58
building techniques, 28

Cajun Louisiana, 25, 40
Cather, Willa, 126
central business district, 78, 92n
Chicago, 77–8, 99
Cincinnati, 34
cityscapes, 73
    ideological aspects, 93n
    influence of government policies, 87
    inner-city decay, 80
    'soft' cities, 120
'Civilized Tribes', 27
classicism, 10
colonial arrivals, 15
commercial strip, 9
Coney Island, 101, 141
conservation issues, 53
convention centres, 82
Creole Louisiana, 25
Crèvecœur, J. Hector, 44n
cultural landscapes
    African-American, 27
    imperial, 27
    plantations, 27
Currier and Ives
    Course of Empire 50, 58, 62, 65, 68

desert, 20; *see also* Mormons
Detroit Renaissance Center, 82–3
development options, 22, 63
Disneyland, 141
Disney World, 9, 141
Dust Bowl, 20, 126, 134

ecological collapse, 24n
ecological niches, 21–3
economic wealth, 1
edge cities, 95
Emerson, Ralph Waldo, 58, 70n
environmental change, 3, 52
expeditions, 19, 65–7
European landscape precedents, 39
ethnic diversity, 45–6, 92n, 132

Farm Security Administration, 72
farming crop yields, 22
fire, 4
forests, 17–18, 134
Four Corners area (south-west), 67
French legacies
    Cajun Louisiana, 40
    long-lots farm, 40
frontier
    hollow frontier, 20, 31
    surveying, 31, 39
frontier settlers
    Germans, 18
    Ulster Scots, 18
frontier thesis,
    Darwinian aspects, 60
    painting aspects, 60
    self-sufficiency, 35

gentrification, 83, 98
geography
    cultural, 5
    physical, 3, 10, 13, 14, 15, 134
geomorphology, 5

Germans, 18, 29, 46
giant redwoods, 23
Glassie, Henry, 128
gold rush, 19
Grand Canyon, 23, 51
Grand Tetons, 52
grasslands, 18
Great American Desert, 19–20
Great Falls of the Potomac, 51
greenfield sites, 80
grid-system land survey, 33–4, 135

heritage
    authenticity problems, 105–6
    disputed sites, 106
    Jamestown Settlement, 106
    Plimoth Plantation, 106
    representation problems, 106
    Virginia Tidewater, 106
High Plains, 14, 19, 20–1, 40, 45
Homestead Act (1862), 22
Hoskins, William G., 121n
houses, 32, 74, 79

imperial legacies, 40
    British, 18, 25–6
    Russian, 25, 135
    Spanish, 25–7, 135
Indian landscapes, 25, 29, 94, 134
inner cities
    decay, 83
    federal policies, 81
    political neglect, 81
    retail redevelopment, 82
    urban developments, 81

Jackson, J. B., 119, 131
James River, 28
Jamestown Settlement, 2, 112
Jefferson, Thomas, 28, 30
    'Empire for Freedom', 10, 67
    estates, 35–6
    'holy agriculture', 36
    Monticello, 35–8
    Northwest Territory, 30, 62
    Notes on Virginia, 16
    organised settlement line, 20
    republican values, 32–3
    University of Virginia, 38

yeoman farmers, 30, 32
Jeffersonian
    rhetoric, 76
    values, 32–3

land
    as commodity, 34
    surveying, 34
landscape
    change, 76–9
    experiences, 62
    images, 62
    methodological issues, 3, 5, 7, 11n,
        142n
    reading skills, 2, 6–7, 136
    record, 2
    settler perceptions, 62
    studying, 3, 5, 7
    term's origins, 36, 63
    variety, 4
    view of the past, 136
landscape in relation to
    access issues, 52–3
    aesthetics, 10, 37, 63, 72, 130
    agrarian ideals, 34–5
    American values, 56, 130–1
    antiquarian traditions, 128
    artefacts, 8, 127
    artistic conventions, 64–6
    choices and constraints, 54n
    commodified images, 62, 68
    cultural discourses, 118
    cultural geography, 124
    cultural history, 128
    cultural perceptions, 137
    cultural signs, 112
    cultural studies, 124
    decoding ideological signs, 129
    democratic values, 119
    discovery, 15
    ecological collapse, 126
    ecological fragility, 20
    ecological variety, 14
    environment, 2
    environmental experience, 133
    environmental issues, 52
    environmental misunderstanding,
        18–19
    environmental perceptions, 125

films, 86
geography, 117
homes and interiors, 28
Hudson River painters, 57–8
human modification, 4
iconography, 69, 72, 84, 131
ideology of progress, 38
images, 16, 62, 73
land policies, 32
literary strategies, 118
luminist tradition, 58
manifest destiny, 56
mapping the West, 33, 40, 42
market economy, 34–5
material culture, 127, 129
memory problems, 110, 112, 136
mental maps, 16, 124
morphological analysis, 8–9
museums' frontier exhibits, 110–11
nature, 52
nostalgia, 68
paintings, 36, 56
Palladian ideals, 37–8
panoramic views, 6
perceptions, 15
physical environment, 13
'plats', 33, 40
post-industrialism, 96–9, 139
post-modern perspectives, 120
prehistory, 15
preservation, 9, 98
prior survey of the West, 33
problematic aspects, 117–21, 132
railroads, transcontinental, 20
regions, 6, 13, 14
relict survivals, 6, 74, 75–6, 94, 129
republican values, 30–1, 39, 88
resources, 45
scenery, 8
self-sufficiency ideals, 35
sense of place, 1–2, 130
sense of wonder, 63–4
social-Darwinism, 45
spectacular landscapes, 59
traditional approaches, 17
urban redevelopment, 95
yeoman farmers, 35
Landscape, 131
landscape studies, 122

Las Vegas, 131
Levittown, 101
Lewis and Clark expedition, 65
log cabin as icon, 31, 135
logging, 3
long-lot land system, 40
Los Angeles, 26, 140
Louisiana Purchase, 27, 29, 40
Lowenthal, David, 125, 136
luminist painting tradition, 58

main street, 9
Making of the English Landscape, 121n, 123, 136
malls see shopping malls
Mammoth Cave, Kentucky, 51
Manhattan, 74, 78, 82, 84–6, 94, 105, 107
manifest destiny, 56
maps and plats, 40, 42
Megalopolis, 75
Meinig, David, 123, 129, 132, 135–6
mental maps, 18
Midwest, 27
  ethnic variety, 45
militia movement, 51
Monticello, 35–8
Monument Valley, 69
  John Ford films, 69
Mormons, 16–17, 26, 47, 129
motorways, 79
museums
  American Museum, Bath, 138, 141
  Ellis Island, 110
  historians' involvement, 111
  material culture, 110
  Museum of American Frontier
    Culture, Staunton, 109
  presentation strategies, 113–14
  Rocky Mount, Tennessee, 110, 113
  Ulster American Folk Park, Omagh,
    109, 111, 138
  US Holocaust Memorial, 110
  Whig view of history, 110

national parks, 53
  Grand Canyon, 51, 62
  Grand Teton, 52
  Yellowstone, 50, 53, 62, 68–9
  Yosemite, 53, 62

native peoples, 15, 25, 27, 67–8, 137
    in folk parks, 112–13
    Pocahontas, 116n
nature
    communing with, 4
    sublime, 52
New England, 9, 75, 134
    as cultural precedent, 31, 39
    diffusion westwards, 26
    townships, 31
New York City, 77, 137
    Brooklyn Bridge, 84–5
    Manhattan skyline, 84, 137
    redevelopment projects, 97
    South Bronx, 83–4
New York upstate, 44n
    Catskills, 4, 58
    Niagara Falls, 9, 59
Niagara Falls, 9, 59, 68, 86, 137
north-east, 75, 77
Northwest Ordinance, 21–2, 31
Northwest Territory, 28, 135

Ohio country, 27, 40, 42, 135
Old Faithful, 9
overgrazing, 3

painters,
    Bierstadt, Albert, 59
    Church, Frederick E., 59
    Cole, Thomas, 57–8
    Cropsey, Jasper, 59
    Durand, Asher B., 58
    Morse, Samuel, 57
paintings
    Kindred Spirits, 58
    Niagara, 59
    The Oxbow, 57
    Storm in the Mountains, 60
panoramas, 6, 11n
Pennsylvania Dutch, see Amish
photographers
    Adams, Ansel, 61, 69
    Hine, Lewis, 87
    Houseman, Thomas, 67
    Jackson, W. H., 67
    Muybridge, Eadwaerd, 67
    O'Sullivan, Timothy, 72
    Riis, Jacob A., 86–7

Pilgrim Fathers, 17
place
    sense of, 1
    attachment, 99n
plantations, 9, 21, 27, 28, 119
    Virginia legacy, 29
Plimoth Plantation, 112
post-modernity, 100n
Puritan communities, 17

religious groups
    Amish, 9, 27
    Mennonites, 27
    Quakers, 27
republican values, 32, 135
Rocky Mountains, 13–14
Romanticism, 4
Russian colonies, 25

scenery, 62
Scotch-Irish see Ulster Scots
Shenandoah Valley, 112–13
shopping malls, 80–2, 90–1, 97
    public access, 83
    West Edmonton Mall, 92n
skyscrapers, 84
Smoky Mountains, 13
sod-busters, 20
soils, 22
southern landscapes
    as western yardstick, 31
    Chesapeake, 27
    southern towns, 74
    south-west, 105, 133, 135
    Texas, 46, 48, 74
Spanish legacy, 16, 114n
Statue of Liberty, 86
Stone Mountain, Georgia, 118
suburbia
    broadening tax base, 81
    developers, 101
    dormitory origins, 81
    economic diversification, 81
    malls, 97
    post-industrial dimensions, 96–9
    processes, 96–7
    Reagan era expansion, 91, 94–5, 140
    related to inner-city decline, 80–1
    saving and loan policies, 79

service industries, 96–7
vernacular aspects, 131–2
white flight to, 96
Sunbelt, 74, 139
surveying, 45
symbolic landscapes, 136
synthetic landscapes, 107–11, 141
 battlefields, 107
 heritage sites, 107–8
 museums, 107
 realistic conventions, 113
 replicas, 108

Texas
 cultural landscapes, 46, 48, 74
 ethnic diversity, 46
theme parks, 92n
 American Adventure, 138
 analyses, 140
 Appalachia, 22
 Barnum pedigree, 114n
 detractors, 103
 Disneyland, 114
 Disney World, 101–10, 114
 Dollywood, 9
 environmental considerations, 114n
 EPCOT, 102, 104, 115n
 Magic Kingdom, 102–3
 Main Street, 103
 Old Dominion, 109
theodolite, 17
Thoreau, Henry, David, 51, 58
topography, 10, 13
topophilia, 63, 125
tourists, 4; see also visitors
Transcendentalism, 4, 52
Trenton Falls, 50
Turner thesis, 45, 76, 105, 113, 125

Ulster Scots, 17, 29
urban change, 76–9
urban icons, 84
used-car lots, 9
US Geological Survey, 68, 72
Utah, 26, 47

van der Rohe, Mies, 117
vernacular landscapes, 9, 119, 128, 130–2
Virginia, 2, 28
 colonial variety, 29–30
 plantation legacy, 29
 Shenandoah Valley, 29, 53
 Tidewater, 21, 28, 29, 30
 Williamsburg, 29
visitors, 93n, 127, 137
 Dickens, Charles, 18, 41, 89
 Mrs Trollope, 18, 34, 89

Walden Pond, 52
Washington DC
 architectural yardstick, 87, 89
 Capitol Hill, 83
 democratic icon, 88
 Federal Triangle, 9, 90–1
 L'Enfant plan, 89
 Mall, the, 2, 90
 planned town, 87, 89
 visitors' accounts, 89
 Watergate redevelopment, 82
weather, 14
Welsh settlers, 43n, 46–7
western frontier, 31
 academic concerns, 105
 frontier thesis see Turner
 Hollywood version, 76, 105
 images, 49, 50, 76
 museum exhibits, 105
westward expansion, 18
Whitman, Walt, 54n
wilderness, 3–4, 23, 29, 53, 137
 as commodity, 68
 image as garden, 41, 49–50, 67
 taming, 32, 62
Wild West, 76
Williamsburg, 29, 30, 109
world fairs, 141

Yellowstone, 68
Yorktown, 109
Yosemite Valley, 9, 68–9

The British Association for American Studies (BAAS)

The British Association for American Studies was founded in 1955 to promote the study of the United States of America. It welcomes applications for membership from anyone interested in the history, society, government and politics, economics, geography, literature, creative arts, culture and thought of the USA.

The Association publishes a newsletter twice yearly, holds an annual national conference, supports regional branches and provides other membership services, including preferential subscription rates to the *Journal of American Studies.*

Membership enquiries may be addressed to the BAAS Secretary, Philip John Davies, Reader in American Studies, School of Humanities, De Montfort University, Leicester LEI 9BH, UK.